Rachel E. Baker

A King's Daughter

A Comedy in three Acts

Rachel E. Baker

A King's Daughter
A Comedy in three Acts

ISBN/EAN: 9783337054984

Printed in Europe, USA, Canada, Australia, Japan

Cover: Foto ©ninafisch / pixelio.de

More available books at **www.hansebooks.com**

A KING'S DAUGHTER

A Comedy in Three Acts

FOR · FEMALE CHARACTERS ONLY

RACHEL

AUTHOR OF " THE CHAP

B

Walter

CHARACTERS.

MRS. GRAHAM.

AUNT CLARISSA.

REBECCA SPENCER, *who thinks herself " one of the girls."*

HELEN GRAHAM, *Mrs. Graham's daughter.*

FLORENCE BALDWIN.

KITTY GREENE.

SALLIE BROWNING, *a " Kodak fiend."*   } *The King's Daughters.*

RUTH ADAMS.

MABEL MORRIS, *whose genius burns.*

POLLY GRAHAM, *who would like to be a King's daughter.*

NAN GRAHAM, *Mrs. Graham's niece.*

Time, the present.   Costumes, modern.

Time in representation, two hours.

Act I. The King's Daughters.

Act II. " In His Name."

Act III. The Fairy Godmother.

A KING'S DAUGHTER.

ACT I.

SCENE. — MRS. GRAHAM'S *drawing-room. Usual furniture. Entrances* C., R., *and* L. *in flat. Window,* R. C.; *fireplace,* R. *in flat;' tea-table, with chair* R. *of it, by fireplace; large table,* R. C.; *chair down* L. *Curtain raised, discovers* HELEN GRAHAM *standing behind table,* R. C., *cutting flannel;* KITTY GREENE *at* R., *seated, sewing;* FLORENCE *at* L., *sewing. Girls laughing and talking.*

KITTY. Won't it be just too jolly for anything?

FLORENCE. The boys have all promised to come.

HELEN. We can have the sale in this room. Mamma is willing. Of course it will be a success, and the society of King's Daughters will be considered a valuable addition to the vast army of charitable institutions.

KITTY. Every town has a band of King's Daughters now. If our work keeps growing, we won't have time for anything else!

HELEN. Never mind. Only think how famous we will be! If a man should meet one of us, he would doff his hat and think, "One of the helpers;" if a woman, she would bow low and say, "Ah, there goes a King's Daughter."

KITTY. Fame is all very well, but it won't mend my clothes. There is an appalling array of repairs awaiting me at home this very moment.

FLORENCE. They should sink into insignificance before the good work you are doing.

KITTY. No sink to them; they float upon the surface of my memory with an " I don't intend to be forgotten " air.

(REBECCA SPENCER *appears at door,* C., *dressed in the extreme of fashion.*)

REBECCA. Ah, how de do girls? Thought I would look in upon you. I am such a creature of impulse, you know.

3

HELEN (*offers chair*). Do sit down, Miss Rebecca. (REBECCA *sits*.) We are very busy, you see. The girls meet here in an hour, and we are preparing the work.

REBECCA. So noble of you, girls. My soul is stirred with an impulse to do noble deeds. It thirsts for them.

FLORENCE. You will be just the one to attend our fair. We are to have a soda fountain, and shall expect that thirst to be allayed.

REBECCA. Ha, ha, how clever you are! I had such a delightful walk this morning. I was wandering in the lane, where the birds were singing and the buds were peeping forth. I am such a creature of impulse, and, being inspired with the dramatic fire of Shakespeare, I took a position like this (*rises, and poses dramatically*), and with a yearning voice spoke thus: "Romeo, Romeo, where art thou, Romeo?" and, *girls*, whom do you think —

KITTY. The Deacon.

REBECCA (*coquettishly*). Yes.

KITTY. Beware, Miss Rebecca. They say that "in spring a young man's fancy lightly turns to thoughts of love."

REBECCA. Ha, ha, you silly creature! The Deacon appeared, and my impulse was to turn and flee, but a little voice within me said, "Faint heart ne'er won —

FLORENCE. A deacon. Ha, ha, Miss Rebecca.

REBECCA (*seated*). I remained, and we walked and talked. (*Sighs*.) Would that I had some noble work to perform.

HELEN (*exchanges glances with the girls*). Why not devote yourself to the Deacon. He leads such a lonely life, poor man.

REBECCA (*sighs*). He does, indeed.

KITTY. What work more noble than to toast his slippers before the open fire ; to caressingly brush his curling locks. Oh, they do curl, Miss Rebecca?

REBECCA (*sighs*). Yes.

KITTY (*rises*). Let me paint a picture for you.

FLORENCE. Why, Kitty Greene! I didn't know that you were an artist.

KITTY (*looks at her with meaning; taps forehead*). The canvas upon which I paint is here. Let me see. A cosey sitting-room like this. (*Becomes dramatic*.) The fast falling snow beats heavily against the casement window. A woman is seated before the cheerful fire. She holds something in her hands. Her eyes have a tender look in them. This something awakens pleasant memories. Her lips are parted in a smile. What can it be? A book? No. A beautiful flower, perhaps, whose fragrance makes glad the heart of the woman? No. What can it be?

REBECCA (*eagerly*). The Deacon's slippers. (*Confused; girls laugh.*)

KITTY. Yes, Miss Rebecca. Then comes a familiar step. The woman rises with outstretched arms, her eyes bright with the light of love, her lips eager to form the words of welcome. (*Girls laugh*.)

REBECCA (*rises*). Nonsense! Your imagination is too vivid, Miss Kitty. Because you are in love, don't think that the whole world will follow you. Paint a picture for me, if you will, but one of noble deeds performed. I envy you. I long to join you in your good work.

HELEN (*crosses to her*). Do you? So glad. I hate to cut out flannel. (*Takes her by arm*.)

KITTY (*same business*). I don't like to baste. You would do it beautifully.

REBECCA (*rises*). Oh, no.

FLORENCE. Your needlework is world-renowned, and I have an important engagement before the meeting.

KITTY. So have I.

HELEN. And so have I. We know of no person more trustworthy.

REBECCA (*retreats toward door*, C.). But I couldn't stop a moment.

GIRLS (*bring her forward*). Oh, yes.

REBECCA (*retreats*). I should spoil it all. ·

GIRLS (*same business*). Oh, no.

KITTY. Just think of the noble deeds!

FLORENCE. No more thirst of soul.

REBECCA (*at door*). Some other time.

HELEN. Your name would live forever.

REBECCA (*with dignity*). The name of Rebecca Spencer will *always* live. (*Exit.*)

FLORENCE (*laughing*). Haven't a doubt of it. It will be Rebecca Spencer to the end of the chapter.

HELEN. Didn't we frighten her? Poor Miss Rebecca. I wish the Deacon would be a creature of impulse and propose to her.

KITTY. It isn't impulse that he needs. It is courage.

FLORENCE. Suppose we turn match-makers, and help them out.

KITTY. How?

FLORENCE. Give me time to concoct a scheme. (*Looking off* L.) Here comes Nan.

HELEN. She will help us with the work.

KITTY. That is hard on Nan. She always helps, and it is generally the part that we don't like.

HELEN (*carelessly*). Oh, she is used to it.

(*Enter* NAN.)

HELEN. We are tired, Nan. You finish the work.

NAN (*quietly*). Very well

HELEN. And be sure and have it ready by three o'clock.

(*Exeunt* FLORENCE *and* HELEN.)

KITTY (*who is still at work*). I think it is mean, Nan, to make you work so hard.

NAN (*at work behind table*). Oh, I am used to it. I haven't any home of my own, you know, and must expect to.

KITTY (*rises*). Don't you get very tired sometimes?

NAN. Yes; very often.

KITTY (*folding work and laying it upon table*). My work is ready. You won't have that to do. (*Arm about* NAN.) I like you, Nan, if you are poor. (*Places small box in* NAN'S *hand.*) Here are some chocolate mints. Good-by. (*Runs off* C.)

NAN. Dear Kitty. She has the right spirit for a King's Daughter, — a loving word for every one. She has given me that which she prizes most, — candy. Will my letter never come? I hardly dare to dream that I shall be fortunate enough to secure an appointment as teacher, and, with it, freedom from dependence — my life and future in my own hands. It makes my heart light to think of it. (*Sings and works. Some one whistles outside.*) There is my faithful swain. (*Runs to window; opens it.*) Good-afternoon, Jack. On your way to school? For me? (*Catches flower, which is thrown into window.*) Oh, thank you. I shall be very proud to wear it. Good-by. (*Waves hand; goes behind table, fastening flower in gown.*) Ever since I nursed Jack through the measles, he has never forgotten me.

(*Enter* POLLY *jumping rope; sees* NAN; *stands upon chair behind her and covers* NAN'S *eyes with her hands.*)

POLLY. Guess.

NAN (*laughing, takes* POLLY'S *hands from her eyes*). I don't need to, Polly, dear. Your voice is such sweet music to my ears, I never forget it. (*Holds up face;* POLLY *kisses her.*) But, my dear child, I thought you were in school.

POLLY (*bringing* NAN *down front*). I was, but I had such a dreadful feeling, I couldn't stand it another moment.

NAN. Why, Polly! Are you suffering?

POLLY. Yes — for cake.

NAN. You witch! You had two pieces this morning.

POLLY. That is just the trouble. It had such a moreish taste, I couldn't stand it.

NAN. Your mother will not be willing for me to give you any more.

POLLY. But I shall. Come.

NAN (*goes back to her work*). I haven't time, Polly. Helen would not like it. There is so much to be done. The King's Daughters will be here soon, and I must have everything ready.

POLLY. Oh, bother the King's Daughters! (*Throws rope around* NAN'S *waist.*) You can't escape me now. Come on, like a lamb led to the slaughter.

NAN. It would be slaughter of cake, if you had your way.

(*Business of dragging* NAN *across stage;* NAN, *with both hands upon rope, resists; finally* POLLY *gains, and both are at door,* L., *laughing; do not see* AUNT CLARISSA, *who tries to enter at same time.*)

AUNT CLARISSA (*assumes harsh manner*). Children! What are you doing? Trying to make a telescope of me?

POLLY. Yes, Aunt Clarissa, if it would bring the cake any nearer.

AUNT C. Well, I never! You are always up to some mischief.

POLLY. Can't help it. Was born with the love of fun — and for cake. Come on, Nan.

NAN. If scoldings follow your third piece of cake, you must not blame me.

(*Exeunt* NAN *and* POLLY.)

AUNT C. Three pieces of cake in one day! When I was a girl, I thought myself lucky to have one piece a month. (*Sits in chair by fireplace.*) Here I am, having thrown myself upon the mercy of relatives who have not seen me for years, alone, without a child, and with more money than I know what to do with. Rather late in life to begin deception, but I must find out which of my nieces would love me for myself. (*Rises and looks at work upon table.*) Making preparations for the King's Daughters. As I profess not to have a penny in the world, I cannot give them money openly, so I will try this little scheme. (*Takes envelope from pocket, puts money into it, writes upon it.*) Where shall I put it? (*Crosses to tea-table.*) Just the place. (SALLIE BROWNING *appears at door,* C., *with Kodak; takes* AUNT CLARISSA'S *picture just as she places envelope upon table; laughs, watches her a moment, then disappears.*) My deception will prove which of my nieces is a King's Daughter at heart. (*Crosses to door,* R.)

(*Enter* MRS. GRAHAM *and* HELEN.)

MRS. GRAHAM. Where are you going, Aunt Clarissa?

AUNT C. (*resumes cross manner*). To my room. I do not wish to be disturbed. (*Exit.*)

HELEN. She must have left her manners at home.

MRS. GRAHAM (*seated at* R. *of table*). I don't know what to do. Your Aunt Clarissa, having lost her money through the unfortunate speculations of some friend, has no home, and must remain with us.

HELEN. The coolest proceeding that I ever heard of. (*Crosses with basket of work to chair down* L.; *sits and works.*) The house isn't large enough as it is. If we keep on, we shall be supporting an asylum for poor relations. There is Nan. She has to be clothed and fed. I don't see why her Uncle John did not leave her some money. Only an old bonnet, which once belonged to his wife. So old-fashioned, it is no earthly good, except for private theatricals.

MRS. GRAHAM. I promised your father that Nan should always have a home. As to giving her the advantages which you and Polly must have, it is simply out of the question. The only thing to do is to give Polly's room to Aunt Clarissa, and you share yours with your sister.

HELEN. Now, Mother Graham, you know that such an idea as that is absurd! Polly is a terror, and so disorderly. I much prefer to room with a cyclone. (POLLY *appears at door*, C., *eating large piece of cake*.) It would be disastrous, but of short duration ; with Polly it would be eternal chaos.

POLLY. That isn't fair, Helen Graham. If you want to call me names, why don't you do it to my face. If I am an "eternal chaos," I don't put on toppy airs, as you do. (*Sits upon table, swings her feet, and eats cake*.)

MRS. G. That will do, Polly. Where did you get that cake?

POLLY. Oh, me and Nan found it.

HELEN. Polly Graham, what language! "Me and Nan."

POLLY. Well, Nan and me, if you like it better.

HELEN. You should say Nan and I.

POLLY (*looks at* HELEN). Any one that is called an "eternal chaos " isn't expected to speak grammatically.

MRS. G. No more of this. The King's Daughters will soon be here, and you ought to be in school.

POLLY. I think it is just as mean as it can be that I can't be a King's Daughter.

HELEN. You are too young, Polly ; you don't know how to sew.

POLLY. Hm! A lot of sewing you girls do. You just meet and pretend to be so busy, but you are talking about people all the time.

MRS. G. When you have finished, Polly, I should like to speak. (POLLY, *very cross, jumps down from table*.) The house is so small, I must give your room to Aunt Clarissa.

POLLY. All right. I can sleep with Nan ; she doesn't call me names.

MRS. G. A happy thought. Yes, that will do nicely. I will attend to it at once. (*Exit*.)

POLLY (*goes behind* HELEN ; *while she is talking, takes ribbon from basket and ties* HELEN *to chair*). Let me join the club, won't you, Helen? I can darn stockings, anyway.

HELEN (*laughing*). If you didn't mend them any better than you do your own, the poor people would all have blistered heels and toes.

POLLY. Nan says that I do them real well, so now!

HELEN. Oh, Nan thinks everything that you do is perfect.

POLLY. Well, *you* don't.

HELEN. Do run away, and don't bother me.

POLLY (*runs to door*, C.). Here they come, the King's.Daughters.

HELEN. I must meet them. (*Tries to rise, but is held by ribbon*.) Why, what is the matter?

POLLY. One, two, three, four of them.

HELEN (*discovers what* POLLY *has done*). Polly Graham, come here this moment and untie me.

POLLY. Couldn't think of it; I might "bother" you.

(*Enter* NAN.)

HELEN. Nan, do come to my rescue.

NAN (*laughing; unties ribbon*). Polly up to pranks again? (HELEN *rises; tries to catch* POLLY, *who dodges behind tables and chairs.*)

POLLY. Take care, Helen; you will make "eternal chaos" of this room.

HELEN. If I catch you, Polly Graham —

POLLY. But you can't. Ha, ha. (*Runs off* C.)

HELEN (*sinks into chair*). That sister of mine will be the death of me. Just because I won't let her join the club.

NAN. Why not? If I understand the true meaning of the name, it is to give help wherever it is needed, whether young or old.

HELEN. I do not wish Polly to join the King's Daughters, and that settles it. (*Rises.*) The next thing we know, *you* will be wanting to join it.

NAN (*bitterly*). Hardly. You never allow me to forget that I am a dependant here; that your mother has given me a home. There is no need for me to join a club, I have plenty of work, as it is.

HELEN. You ought to be very thankful that you have a home.

NAN (*looks at her*). I am — very. (AUNT CLARISSA *heard outside calling*, "*Nan, Helen, Polly.*")

HELEN. There is that amiable Aunt Clarissa. I wish that she had concluded to visit some of her other relatives.

(*Enter* AUNT CLARISSA.)

AUNT C. Oh, there you are. A pretty time I have had of it. Helen, find my glasses.

HELEN. Indeed! What right have you to order me about? If you wish to live with us, you must find your own glasses.

AUNT C. Well, I never! A chit of a girl like you to talk in this way. Nan!

NAN (*crosses to her*). Yes, Aunt Clarissa; here they are. (*Glasses have been hanging down* AUNT CLARISSA'S *back; leads her to chair by table.*)

AUNT C. I need to have a pair of eyes in the back of my head. (*Wiping glasses.*) Your mother says that company is coming.

HELEN. *I* am to have company. The King's Daughters.

AUNT C. You don't say so. Royalty?

HELEN (*shows annoyance*). No; a club of young ladies. They meet and work for charity.

AUNT C. A fashionable fad. Hm!

HELEN. You must not sneer like that; we do a great deal of good.

AUNT C. It would be better if *you* did more work at home.

HELEN. It isn't necessary. We have Nan to help us.

AUNT C. Oh, yes. It is " Nan " here and " Nan " there, all the day.

HELEN. You call upon Nan just as much as the rest of us.

NAN (*at door* C.). Please do not make me a topic of conversation. Some one is coming.

HELEN (*runs to door*). It is Sallie Browning. Be sure and have everything ready, Nan. (*Exit.*)

NAN (*comes down*). Aunt Clarissa, I will find your glasses, bring to you anything you may wish, only don't, please, talk of me to Helen.

AUNT C. Why do you allow her to impose upon you?

NAN. I cannot help myself. I am a dependant here. Aunt Graham has given me a home.

AUNT C. Didn't your Uncle John leave you any of his money?

NAN. I am afraid not. He was eccentric, you know. They have not found his will yet. Just before he died he gave me such a queer legacy.

AUNT C. What was it?

NAN. Only an old bonnet which belonged to his wife. He told me it would shelter my head from the storms. I shall never part with it, of course, but it is useless.

AUNT C. Can you show it to me?

NAN. Certainly. I won't be a moment. (*Exit.*)

AUNT C. Just like a man. The idea of giving anything like that to a young girl!

(*Enter* NAN, *wearing old-fashioned bonnet; kneels beside* AUNT C.)

NAN. " Dost like the picture?"

AUNT C. Hm! A fashion of fifteen years ago. Why don't you do something to make yourself independent? There are plenty of ways for one to earn a living.

NAN (*eagerly*). If you will promise not to breathe a word of it, I will tell you a secret.

AUNT C. You will find me like the contribution box — ready to receive, but no returns.

NAN (*after looking cautiously about*; HELEN *enters* C.; *stops to listen*). I have studied every night for the past year in my own room after my work was done, and have passed the examinations successfully. I am only waiting for an appointment as teacher. The mail may bring it any day. Only think of it, Aunt Clarissa, to take care of myself — to be out in the world, away from Helen's tyranny. I hardly dare dream of such happiness. (*Girls heard outside laughing.*) Not a word, remember. (HELEN *exit.*)

AUNT C. (*wipes her eyes*). I am glad of it.

NAN (*looks at her in surprise*). Why, Aunt Clarissa! Tears in your eyes for me?

AUNT C. (*resumes sharp tone, and rises*). Mind your business, you hussy, and take me to my room!

NAN (*gives her arm to* AUNT CLARISSA). Ha, ha, auntie. You can't deceive me. Your bark is worse than your bite. (*They exeunt* R., AUNT CLARISSA *shaking her head.*)

(HELEN *and* SALLIE BROWNING *appear at door* C., *their backs turned to audience.* SALLIE *has a Kodak, and is taking some one's picture.* *Snaps Kodak.*)

SALLIE. Ha, ha. I have him. Poor little fellow. See him run. Evidently he thinks that that snap means powder. (*Girls enter.*)

HELEN. Sallie, you are a perfect fiend with that Kodak! Every man, woman, and child will have, had their pictures taken before the summer is over.

SALLIE. Of course they will. What is a Kodak for, if not to make your friends miserable.

HELEN. I haven't a doubt but you will make its mission a successful one.

SALLIE (*points Kodak at* HELEN). And you shall lead the procession.

HELEN (*moving out of range*). Thanks, but I decline the honor.

SALLIE (*places Kodak upon table*). Here I am arrayed in war-paint and feathers for the massacre of flannel. Bring on the victims.

(*Enter* KITTY *and* RUTH.)

KITTY. Hallo, girls!

RUTH. What do we work upon to-day? (*All the girls have sewing-bags; take off hats and coats.*)

(*Enter* NAN.)

SALLIE. Here's Nan. (*Girls group about* NAN, *who takes their coats and hats.*)

KITTY (*noticing flower which* NAN *wears*). Nan has a sweetheart. Come, confess.

NAN (*laughing*). No secret. My lover is four feet in height, and twelve years old.

KITTY. Rapid youth. He is beginning young. Who is it?

NAN. You will be jealous when I tell you.

KITTY. I am green now with jealousy.

NAN (*shaking finger at* KITTY). It won't be Kitty *Greene* long, from all I hear.

GIRLS. O Kitty, do tell us!

SALLIE. Are you engaged?

KITTY. No, I am not. Don't you see that Nan is trying a game of bluff? We will pursue you, Nan, so be honest.

NAN. We will spare you this time, Miss Kitty. My admirer is Johnny Mullen. I call him Jack for short. He has been my devoted admirer ever since I helped him through the measles. He thinks that I saved his life. (*At door ; laughs.*) You see, my romance cannot prove a very serious one.

RUTH. Oh, dear! I wish *somebody* I knew would have the measles.

KITTY. Think of Tom Mason having the measles! (*Girls laugh.*)

HELEN (*arm about* RUTH). You and Tom seem to be getting on finely without the measles. Come. girls, get to work.

SALLIE (*girls seated*). Beth Hamlin and Mabel Morris are not here yet.

RUTH. Where is Florence Baldwin?

HELEN. She will soon be here. She has something on her mind.

RUTH. Is she in love?

KITTY. For mercy sakes, Ruth Adams! Don't think because you have a man on *your* mind, every one else has.

HELEN (*distributing pieces of flannel to girls*). We work to-day for Mrs. Mullen and her family. We are to make flannel skirts.

FLORENCE. I hope it won't be anything that needs hemming. I detest it.

SALLIE. I had much rather hem than gather.

KITTY (*looking in bag*). I do believe that I have forgotten my thimble. Never could sew without one.

SALLIE. Kitty is trying to crawl. Helen has an extra one, I know.

HELEN. Yes, I will find one. (*Calls, "Nan," at door ; comes down.*) Here comes Florence. (*Enter* FLORENCE, *running.*)

FLORENCE. O girls! I have the best scheme.

GIRLS. What is it?

FLORENCE (*sits*). Let me get my breath first. You know Deacon Starr. Well, he is a bachelor.

KITTY. As he has lived a bachelor in this town ever since we were born. that is not very startling news, and not worth losing one's breath for.

FLORENCE. Do wait and let me finish. Then, there is Rebecca Spencer, spinster.

KITTY (*with sarcasm*). More news. Florence, you are a wonder.

FLORENCE. I propose that the King's Daughters shall do some match-making.

GIRLS (*interested*). What do you mean?

FLORENCE. Let us get to work, and I will tell you. -

(Enter NAN.*)*

NAN. Did you call me, Helen?

HELEN. Yes ; Kitty has forgotten her thimble. Will you bring mother's?

NAN. Certainly. (*Turns to leave the room.*)

SALLIE. Oh, dear! I haven't a needle. Nan, will you please bring me a needle?

FLORENCE. My scissors are too dull for anything. A pair of scissors, please.

NAN. Don't you think that I had better bring some thread?

HELEN. Yes; Sallie will need it when she gathers. (SALLIE *groans;* NAN *exit.*) We must be more careful about our sewing, girls. (*Takes notes from pocket.*) Here is a note from Mrs. Brady. (*Reads.*) "Dear Miss, — The little shirts yees made for the boys was just illegant. Only, would yees moind (I axes yees pardon for my boldness), plaze, wid the nixt ones sind some sthrong thread, for the stitches don't hold together." (*Girls laugh.*)

FLORENCE. That is a hint at our sewing.

HELEN (*reads another note*). Here is one from Mrs. Murphy: "Dear Miss, — Shure, if yees don't moind, will yees make the binding of the shirts for the baby a little larger. At prisent, whin the dear darlint lies down, he has to sit up, the neck is so tight."

(GIRLS *laugh.*)

KITTY. That young hopeful will be a stockbroker when he grows up. He believes in a margin.

SALLIE. Now tell us your scheme, Florence.

GIRLS. Oh, yes.

FLORENCE. We all know that Deacon Starr has loved Rebecca Spencer for years, but hasn't the courage to offer himself. Now I think it would be a kindness to help them.

RUTH. Just what our club is for.

KITTY (*thinks a moment*). The Deacon is too old for measles. Couldn't work that.

FLORENCE. Let us make the Deacon jealous. We will send Miss Rebecca a love letter from some unknown admirer, and the Deacon shall hear of it.

HELEN. We can have a post-office at our sale.

FLORENCE. Good — just the thing.

(Enter NAN *with basket of sewing materials.*)

NAN. For fear that some one had forgotten something else, here is a full supply, from the finest cotton (*laughs and looks at* FLORENCE) for hemming —

FLORENCE (*sighs*). Oh, dear!

NAN (*looks at* SALLIE). To the strongest for gathering.

SALLIE (*sighs*). Oh, dear!

NAN. No excuse for any one now.

RUTH. Why don't you join our club, Nan?

NAN (*exchanges glances with* HELEN). Oh, I am — too busy.

HELEN. Yes, Mamma could not very well spare her. She must be wanting you *now*, Nan.

NAN (*with meaning*). Yes, *my* charity begins at home. (*Exit* L.)

FLORENCE. I thought that Nan was your cousin, Helen?

(POLLY *appears at door* C.)

HELEN. Only a very distant one.

POLLY (*whistles*). Well, I never!

HELEN. Polly, it isn't good form to whistle.

POLLY. It isn't "good form" to tell fibs. Nan is our first cousin, and you know it. She is just as good as we are, if she is poor. She doesn't sew for poor people, but she helps them, just the same. When Mrs. Mullen's children were sick, Nan went down there at night after her work was done and took care of them. Distant cousin! She is such a *near* cousin that life wouldn't be worth living without her.

HELEN. You probably won't be deprived of your incentive to live. Nan won't leave us in a hurry.

POLLY. I don't know about that. (*Holds up letter.*) This looks suspicious.

RUTH (*rises*). A love letter! Do let me see the handwriting.

POLLY (*waves her aside*). What, make my Nan's secrets public property? Never!

(MABEL MORRIS *and* BETH HAMLIN *run in* C.)

HELEN. Why, girls, you are late.

MABEL. "Late!" Good. Just the word I have been trying to find. (*Comes down to front of stage; takes paper from pocket; writes.*)

FLORENCE. Struggling with poetry again, Mab?

BETH. I should think so. I couldn't get a word out of her all the way

MABEL. Yes, I have been working for hours upon just four lines.

SALLIE (*takes up Kodak*). What! You working, Mab? I must have your picture. (*Snaps Kodak.*) Let's hear the poetry, Mab.

MABEL. You will make fun of it.

FLORENCE. Never.

MABEL (*starts to read*). You will laugh.

RUTH. Not a smile.

MABEL (*reads*).

> "Hurrah! for genius that sleeps in my pate.
> To be a fine poet is surely my fate.
> Dear Muse, a laggard I very much hate.
> Awake from thy slumbers before 'tis too late."

(GIRLS *applaud.*)

KITTY. Wait until we hear that slumbering lion roar. I hope you will keep him chained.

SALLIE. Doesn't your head ever ache? I should think so much pent-up genius would make it heavy.

MABEL (*stands defiant with hands folded*). That is right. Make me a target for your shots. I can stand the volley.

(*Enter* POLLY.)

HELEN. Why don't you write a story, Mab?

MABEL (*seated*). I intend to some time. These are only pot-boilers.

POLLY. What is a pot-boiler?

MABEL. My first attempts. They light the flame of genius.

(*Enter* MRS. GRAHAM.)

MRS. G. Good-afternoon, girls. (GIRLS *rise and shake hands with her; she looks at work.*) You are really accomplishing something. Mrs. Mullen will be, or ought to be, a very happy mother to have so many stitches taken for her. You must be tired.

FLORENCE. We are. Isn't it time to take a rest?

SALLIE. Yes, let us bid good-by to work.

KITTY. All right; I am with you. (GIRLS *place work upon table.*)

HELEN. I will show you the things for the fair while we are waiting for the tea. Polly, you may light the kettle on the tea-table. (MABEL *drops paper of poetry on floor;* GIRLS *exeunt with* MRS. GRAHAM, *laughing and talking.*)

POLLY. I am allowed the pleasure of lighting the lamp. (*Bows profoundly.*) King's Daughters, I appreciate the honor, and in consequence shall feel toppy for the rest of the day. (*Walks about room with dignity; sings to air of* "*I'm so happy, I'm so happy,*" — "*I'm so toppy, I'm so toppy.*") I wonder where the matches are. (*Picks up paper from floor.*) Mab's poetry! Just the thing. She uses it to light the flame of genius, why not as good for alcohol? (*Unseen by audience, lights paper with match and lights lamp.*) That ought to be soothing tea. So much slumbering genius. (*Takes letter from pocket.*) Nan's letter. She shall have it at once. I think it is from the school committee. Hope it brings good news. (*Starts to put letter in pocket; drops it on floor.*) I have an idea. (*Takes plate of cake from tea-table.*) I will take this cake to Mrs. Mullen. If I can't sew for her, I can give her something to eat. It will do the King's Daughters good to deny themselves something for sweet charity. Ha, ha, won't Helen be just furious. It will be too late. While she is giving vent to her wrath, the five little Mullens will be sitting in a row devouring the cake. If I can't be a King's Daughter *one* way, I will another. (*Exit* C. *with plate of cake.*)

(*Enter* HELEN.)

HELEN. I wonder if Polly lighted the lamp. (*Crosses to tea-table.*) Yes, and the water will soon be boiling. (*Sees .letter on floor; picks it up.*) A letter for Nan, and in a man's handwriting. From whom can it be? I should like to know. Her appointment as teacher, perhaps. It is not closely sealed. (*Looks cautiously about.*) Nan need never know. (*Opens letter.*) No, much as I would like to read it, I will not stoop to so base an act. Nan a teacher! She would leave here, and become independent. She has made a secret of this. The idea of taking such a step without consulting us! I will have a secret, too, Miss Nan, just long enough to make it too late for your appointment. You will find it isn't wise to have secrets from me. (GIRLS *heard laughing*; HELEN *puts letter in pocket and calls* " *Girls* " *at door* C.)

(*Enter* GIRLS.)

HELEN. The tea is not quite ready. Suppose we rehearse our song for the fair.
GIRLS. Oh, yes!
HELEN. The costumes are all ready in my room. (GIRLS *rush to door* R. *and exeunt laughing.*)

(*Enter* NAN.)

NAN (*moves table to back of room while talking*). Oh, if that letter would only come! If they only knew how anxious I am to be free and independent — to take myself from here where everything is a constant reminder that I am poor! No, I must not say every-thing, for Polly's love has been the one bright spot in my weary life. Her laugh is the sunshine; her true heart keeps mine from losing courage. Why has fate been so unkind to me? Surely, I am as deserving as Helen, yet all the good things come to her, while I must not even dream of such pleasures. (*Sits at table; leans head upon hands.*)

(*Enter* POLLY, C.)

POLLY. Talk about my fondness for cake! Those little Mullenses would breed a famine in a pastry shop. Why, Nannie dear, what is the matter?
NAN (*wiping eyes*). Nothing, dear. I lost my courage just for a moment.
POLLY. I almost forgot. ⅃ have a letter for you. (*Puts hand in pocket.*)
NAN (*rising quickly*). A letter? Oh, give it to me, Polly.
POLLY. I will just as soon as I can find it. (*Takes from pocket three handkerchiefs, hair ribbon, and gloves.*) Dear me! I hope I haven't lost it.

NAN (*eagerly*). I hope not. Look again, Polly.

POLLY (*goes over same business*). No, I must have dropped it when I went to the Mullenses. I'll just fly. (*Makes for door* C.; *stops and comes down again.*) Oh, Nan! I just met the little lame girl, Mollie Grant. She was crying.

NAN. Crying? Did you ask her why?

POLLY. Yes; and she said that the school committee had taken away her sister's appointment.

NAN (*indignantly*). Oh, that is a shame. She is the only support of her family.

POLLY. I told her that you would run over and see them. You always help people when they are in trouble. (*Arm around her.*) Don't lose courage again, will you, Nan? When you cry, it takes a piece of my heart right out. I'll come right back. (*Runs out door* C.)

NAN. The Grants are in trouble again. The committee ought to be more thoughtful. When I dare to dream of the happiness such an appointment may bring to me, I can realize what the disappointment must be to Janet Grant. I will go to her at once. Perhaps I can help her. (*Exit* C.)

(*Enter* GIRLS *dressed in white students' caps and gowns. They wear the silver cross and purple ribbon. They stand in line at back of stage.* GIRL *in* C. *sings solo; others join in refrain and chorus.*)

Six little maids stand in a row.
(*Refrain;* GIRLS *courtesy.*) The King's Daughters.
Dressed in the cap and gown, you know.
The King's Daughters.
Happy is the girl who joins our band,
And lends to all a helping hand.
We meet together to work and sew.
Then take a rest like *this*, you know.

(GIRLS *join hands and walk to front of stage during chorus.*)

(*Chorus.*) Gayly we laugh and sing
Through the long day;
Loud do our voices ring,
We feel so gay.
We are a merry band
Of maids to see.
Helpers in this our land,
You will agree.

(*End* GIRLS *turn, separate, and march toward back of stage, followed by the others, meeting in* C., *ready for second verse.*)

Six little gowns of snowy white.
The King's Daughters.
Their praises we can all indite.
The King's Daughters.
Grateful are many, who know us well,
Of kindly deeds, each one can tell.
Six royal daughters we are, you know.
Our motto "Do good, where'er you go."

(*Chorus.*)   Gayly we laugh and sing. Etc.

Six little caps on six little heads.
            The King's Daughters,
We love to help with needles and threads.
            The King's Daughters.
Three cheers for the maids with caps and gowns,
Three cheers for the girls in all the towns,
Who think of the poor in every land
And give to each a helping hand.

(*Chorus.*)   Gayly we laugh and sing. Etc.

(GIRLS *at back of stage take off caps and gowns, talking and laughing together.*)

(NAN *enters.*)

KITTY.   I am as hungry as a bear.

FLORENCE.   So am I.

HELEN (*seated at tea-table, serving tea;* NAN *passes cups*). Why, Nan, you have forgotten the cake.

NAN.   I think not.   It was there early in the afternoon.

HELEN.   More of Polly's mischief, I am sure.

POLLY (*appears at window*).   Shouldn't wonder.   It has gone, alas, to nourish the struggling lives of the five little Mullenses.   I thought they ought to have something.   It will be the glorious Fourth of July before those flannel skirts will be ready.

SALLIE.   You are a born prophet, Polly.

HELEN.   She is a born tease.

MABEL.   I wonder where my poetry is ?

HELEN (*takes burnt paper from tea-table*).   What is this, Mab?

MABEL (*takes paper*).   My poetic effusion.   Some one has been cruel enough to use it to light the lamp.

POLLY.   You called it a "pot-boiler."   It has made a fine water-boiler.   (MABEL *rushes to window;* POLLY *disappears laughing.*)

FLORENCE.   I do hope we will have a fine day for our fair.   Who will tell fortunes ?

SALLIE.   I will, by palmistry.   My imagination is vivid.   What I don't see, I shall invent.

MABEL.   If you don't find literary lines in my hand, I shall cease to write.

FLORENCE.   There, Sallie!   Here is a chance for you to do good to suffering humanity.   What you don't see, don't invent.

MABEL (*rises*).   I know I have talent.   I feel it

When my thoughts do upward soar,
Away from brooks and grassy lea,
Genius comes knocking at my door
And whispers gently —

HELEN (*presents cup*).   Have some tea.   (GIRLS *laugh.*)

HELEN (*laughing*).   Couldn't resist the temptation, Mab.   It was too good an opportunity to lose.

(*Enter* NAN *with plate of cakes; passes it to* GIRLS.)

HELEN. Isn't it mean? All the new teachers at the high school (NAN *starts;* HELEN *watches her*) are strangers. (NAN *drops plate.*) Why, Nan, how awkward!

NAN (*picks up plate*). I am very sorry. I felt dizzy for a moment.

HELEN. The committee have not made a single appointment in town.

KITTY. Isn't that a shame? So many will be disappointed.

NAN. Oh, there must be some mistake. They surely could not be so unkind.

HELEN. Any one would think, to hear you talk, that it was of vital importance to you.

NAN. Oh, no. I — I always feel deeply for the unsuccessful candidate. (*Brushes hand across eyes.*)

(*Enter* POLLY.)

POLLY. I can't find your letter anywhere. Has any one seen a letter for Nan, which I dropped?

HELEN (*takes up envelope from table*). What is this? ?

POLLY. Give it to me.

HELEN. Not so fast, my dear. (*Reads envelope;* AUNT CLARISSA *appears at door* C.) "From one who desires to help the King's Daughters in their good work."

KITTY. A fairy in disguise hovers near us.

AUNT C. (*comes down*). What is it?

HELEN (*taking money from envelope*). A ten-dollar bill. Who could have given it to us?

SALLIE. Have you a rich aunt, Helen?

HELEN (*laughs*). Rich? Only so far as to have a wealth of relatives to live upon.

(AUNT C. *pained; turns away.*)

POLLY. Don't go, Aunt Clarissa. Sit down and have a cup of tea. (*Leads* AUNT C. *to chair near tea-table.*) It isn't every family that is fortunate enough to have a dear old lady come and live with them. (*Gives tea to* AUNT C.) Helen Graham, I am ashamed of you. You may be a King's Daughter in *name* but not at *heart*.

HELEN. Excuse my sister, girls. She is fond of giving me a curtain lecture. Let's talk about the fair.

SALLIE. We must have a candy table. Who will take charge of that?

BETH. I will. We will have some home-made candies. I have fine receipts.

SALLIE. All right, Beth. (*Writes on paper.*) Down you go.

RUTH. I shall be devoted to your corner, Beth.
FLORENCE. Does Tom like candy, Ruth?
RUTH. Some kinds.
MABEL. Kisses? (GIRLS *laugh.*)
FLORENCE. We must have a post-office.

(*During this conversation* POLLY *tries to get a piece of cake;* HELEN *will not give it to her.*)

(*Enter* REBECCA SPENCER.)

REBECCA. Having a cup of tea? (*No one speaks.*) Having a cup of tea? (*Comes down to tea-table.*)
POLLY (*laughing*). Not having, Miss Rebecca, but have had a cup of tea. Sorry you came too late.
HELEN. It took us so long to cut out the flannel, Miss Rebecca, we required more than one cup to sustain us.
SALLIE. It was delicious tea. Just the kind you prefer, I am sure.
REBECCA. I was walking by, and, being a creature of impulse, you know, thought I would look in upon you.
FLORENCE. You still thirst for something. This, you see, is the reward for doing good. Had you remained with us, it would have been your privilege to drink of the fountain which for the nonce cheers the despondent soul.
MABEL (*clasps hands*). Hear, hear!
FLORENCE. No flowers, ladies.
POLLY (*at window*). Some one is coming down the street. No — yes, it is —
REBECCA. The Deacon?
POLLY. Yes; with what a stately air he walks! How eagerly he looks, now to the right, now to the left! He must be expecting some one.
KITTY. Why don't you run and meet him, Polly? He likes to talk with you.
POLLY. I will. (*Makes for door.*)
REBECCA (*holds her back*). You will do nothing of the kind. I will meet the Deacon, and if I am too late here, I will have some tea at my own fireside, and in better company.
KITTY. Shall you serve toast?
REBECCA (*at door* C.). Toasted what?
KITTY. Slippers. (GIRLS *laugh;* MISS REBECCA *exit with dignity.*)
POLLY. Give me a piece of cake, Helen.
HELEN. No, I will not.
POLLY. I *will* have a piece of your old cake, you see if I don't. (*Exit.*)
FLORENCE. The mystery does not seem to be solved about our gift of money.

AUNT C. I should not try to. The donor doubtless has good reasons for giving anonymously.

KITTY. Perhaps it was you, Aunt Clarissa.

HELEN. Ha, ha, Kitty! You don't know what you are talking about.

AUNT C. (*aside*). You certainly do not.

SALLIE. It is too bad that Nan's letter should be lost. I don't believe she has so many, that she cares to lose one.

HELEN (*carelessly*). It will turn up in time. Such things always do.

(*Enter* NAN.)

NAN. There is an old woman at the gate. She is asking for help.

AUNT C. Here is an opportunity for the King's Daughters to show how much good they can do.

KITTY. Do have her come in, Helen. It will be great fun.

SALLIE. I hope she won't like cake. (*Eating a piece.*) This is too good to give away.

HELEN. Show her in, Nan. (NAN *exit.*) I haven't a doubt but she is some impostor. Now, girls, we must be very dignified.

KITTY. Don't give her any of your poetry, Mab; she wouldn't appreciate it.

SALLIE. I must have her picture. (*Takes Kodak.*)

(*Enter* NAN *leading* POLLY, *who is dressed in long black cloak, black bonnet with veil over face.*)

NAN. I think she must be very deaf; she doesn't hear very well. (*Seats her in chair, placed in* C. *of stage by* HELEN; GIRLS *grouped about her.*)

AUNT C. She must be very tired.

HELEN (*to* POLLY). Have you travelled far?

POLLY (*disguises voice*). What say?

HELEN (*raising voice*). Have you come from a distance?

POLLY. Oh, yes; I walked ten miles.

SALLIE. Poor old lady!

HELEN. Would you like a cup of tea?

POLLY. What say?

HELEN. I shall need a new voice, if she remains here long. Would you like a cup of tea?

POLLY. Something stronger. (GIRLS *look at one another with astonishment.*)

AUNT C. Well, I never!

HELEN. She cannot have anything stronger than coffee. (*To* POLLY.) Will you have some coffee?

POLLY. Cup of coffee?

HELEN. Yes.

POLLY (*nods head*). Yes, coffee.

HELEN. Nan, do get her a cup of coffee. (NAN *exit.*)
POLLY. I would like some cake.
FLORENCE. Well, I never!

(HELEN *offers cake, which* POLLY *takes and eats.*)

POLLY. I heerd tell how the king and his darters was a-stopping here. Thought I'd call.
KITTY. Oh, this is a friendly call. (GIRLS *laugh.*)
POLLY. Be you the girls?
HELEN. Yes, there are six of us.
POLLY. Be they? I knew your father once. He and me was old friends.
FLORENCE (*taps forehead*). Something wrong here.
KITTY. Perhaps she is suffering from pent-up genius. Look out, Mab, it is dangerous.
POLLY. Some more cake, please. (GIRLS *look at one another, as* HELEN *passes cake.*) I thought I'd come and stop a spell.
HELEN. No, that is impossible. The house is full now.
AUNT C. Yes, with poor relations. (AUNT C. *and* HELEN *exchange glances; both spiteful.*)

(*Enter* MRS. GRAHAM.)

MRS. G. What is all this commotion?
HELEN. An old lady. She seems to have lost her way. (NAN *enters with coffee.*)
MRS. G. (*comes down; looks at* POLLY; *puts on glasses*). It seems to me that I have seen that cloak before. (*Looks more closely.*) Surely, I know that bonnet. Yes, and this is my veil. (*Raises veil;* POLLY *discovered laughing.*)
HELEN. Polly Graham!
POLLY (*holds up cake*). It is good cake, Helen.

(*Tableau:* POLLY *in* C. *of stage, eating cake and laughing at* HELEN; NAN *at her* L., *offering cup of coffee;* AUNT CLARISSA *standing by tea-table, hands raised in astonishment;* GIRLS *grouped about* POLLY *laughing;* SALLIE *takes* POLLY'S *picture.*)

QUICK CURTAIN.

ACT II.

"IN HIS NAME."

SCENE.— *Same as in Act I. Time, two days later. Tables on either side of the room with framework of wood above them. Flower-booth at back, C. of stage. Framework of tables draped. The King's Daughter's cross made of silver paper above each table.* HELEN *discovered sitting upon top of steps, arranging drapery and cross of table down* R.; KITTY *standing upon chair before table down* L., *hanging fancy articles upon wire above table;* GIRLS *moving about, arranging tables. As curtain is raised, all singing chorus, "Gayly we laugh and sing," etc.*

KITTY. Helen dear, do deign to look down from your lofty perch and tell me how this array of infants' sacks strikes your artistic eye.

HELEN. Lovely, Kitty! It is a tempting display. Any baby in town, that doesn't possess one of those sacks, will raise its voice in protest.

SALLIE. If you have any regard for the peace and happiness of *my* family, don't let our baby see one of them. He protests enough as it is.

FLORENCE. You ought to be ashamed of yourself, Sallie Browning, to talk so about that small brother of yours. He is a dear. What shall we do with the money we make at this sale? I wish we could found an institution that would live forever.

BETH (*comes down with toy horses*). My vote would be a hospital for maimed and invalid horses.

SALLIE. Yes, and in ten days that worthy representative which you hold in your hand, after being in the possession of some small boy, would be crippled for life and ready to join your ranks.

HELEN. I think it would be fine to do great things and make your mark in the world.

(*Enter* POLLY, C., *with large piece of cardboard, upon which is partially printed "The King's Daughters."* POLLY *wears long-sleeved apron, which is covered with black paint; paint upon hands and face.*)

POLLY. Well, I've made mine.

HELEN. Why, Polly Graham! You are paint from head to foot.

POLLY. Don't you suppose I know it? How would you have me paint, from foot to head? I have been working all the morning on the old thing, and there is more paint on me than there is on the card.

KITTY. We shall put you under a glass case and label you " Our black diamond."

POLLY (*shaking steps upon which* HELEN *is seated*). Come down and help me, Helen. I shall never get the old thing done.

HELEN. Stop shaking these steps. If you are not careful I shall fall and make my mark on your head.

POLLY. It wouldn't be the first time you had tried to *sit* upon me.

KITTY (*arm about* POLLY). Oh, come, Polly, no pouts to-day. I will help you. You are getting on finely.

POLLY (*holds out apron*). You mean my apron is. (POLLY *and* KITTY *exeunt.*)

HELEN. What shall we have for a post-office ?

FLORENCE. Nan is looking for something. Mab is writing the letters. (GIRLS *laugh outside.*) There she is now. From the laughter, I should judge they are having great sport.

(*Enter* MABEL *and* RUTH, *laughing.*)

RUTH. Oh, girls, such fun! If Rebecca Spencer does not think herself devotedly loved, it won't be Mab's fault.

HELEN. Do read it to us.

RUTH. Yes, it is too good to keep.

MABEL. Only upon one condition. That you each promise to make me your private secretary in all matters of love.

GIRLS. Oh, yes!

MABEL (*reads*). "Dear Madam, — Does not your fluttering heart tell you that I am near ? " (*Speaks.*) How is that?

GIRLS. Good ! Go on.

MABEL (*reads*). "As you wander in the woodland, does not the opening bud, the sweet carolling bird tell you that I love you ?" (*Speaks.*) Carolling bird is good, if I did write it. (*Reads.*) "Alas! I know that for years you have loved another, yet the hope burns in my breast" —

FLORENCE. I hope it won't cause spontaneous combustion.

MABEL (*reads*). "That as he has not the courage to speak, you will at least consider this tender offer, which comes from the depths of my yearning heart.

Yours, until death,

ROMEO."

HELEN. Ha, ha, Mab ! That is immense.

FLORENCE. What about the Deacon ?

MABEL. I have one for him as well. (*Reads.*) "Dear Sir, — My natural modesty and delicacy prompt me to write this letter. I know that you love and have loved for years Miss Rebecca Spencer of this town. Yet why this long silence ? I will wait no longer. I, too, love this fair maiden, and have told her of my love. Bid farewell to your fondest hopes. I now await the answer of one who, with her grace and beauty, for me turns darkness into light, sadness into joy. Adieu, and think of me as one who will possess the heart and hand of the woman, who, but for want of courage, might have been yours. From one that loves Rebecca."

HELEN. Bravo! I am proud of you, Mab.

MABEL. We must address them.

(FLORENCE *brings small table to front of stage ; one of the girls brings writing-materials.*)

MABEL (*seated writing*). They tell me that my writing is masculine enough.

SALLIE. You must not write them both alike.

MABEL. The angular style will do for one.

SALLIE (*looking over her shoulder*). Why, Mab! You are only making diagonal lines.

MABEL. Well, Sallie Browning! If your eyes haven't been educated to the angular style of handwriting, you had better give up charity work and devote the time to your education.

SALLIE. But I can't read it.

MABEL. That is all right. Only one of the characteristics of the angular hand.

(*Rises ;* GIRLS *remove tables ; enter* NAN *with box with compartments for letter box.*)

NAN. Will this do?

FLORENCE. Just the thing. Where shall we have it, girls?

SALLIE (*at table back of stage*). This is a good place. (NAN *places box upon it.*)

MABEL. We will put these letters in the box. (*Puts letters in post-office.*)

NAN (*coming down to table* L). How are you getting on? Can I help you?

FLORENCE (*who is winding cheese-cloth around legs of table, which is afterward to be covered by falling drapery*). Yes, I wish you would help me here.

NAN. Certainly. (*Helps her.*) This leg is wet with glue ; woe unto the one that makes a resting place of it.

FLORENCE. We had better engage Polly to paint a sign, " Look out for glue."

HELEN. I have finished using the steps, Nan. You may take them away. (NAN *does not answer.*) Did you hear, Nan?

NAN. Yes ; but I am busy at present.

(POLLY *enters.*)

HELEN. No matter if you are. When I tell you to do anything, I expect it done at once.

POLLY. Oh, you do, Miss Graham! Nan, don't you stir one step. Let Helen wait upon herself. (NAN *makes no answer, but goes.towards steps ;* POLLY *stands in front of her.*) Nan Graham, if you touch those steps, I will never forgive you.

NAN (*puts her gently aside, takes up steps*). Yes, Polly, you will. Remember, I know my duty better than you. (*Arm about* POLLY, *draws her down to front of stage.*) And be patient. Do not forget what the future may have in store for me. (*Exit* L., *with steps.*)

POLLY. I hope the time will come, Helen Graham, when you will have to ask Nan's pardon on bended knee. (*Throws herself upon floor and leans against leg of table wet with glue.*)

FLORENCE. Oh, Polly! That is all —

HELEN (*interrupts her; aside*). Let her find it out for herself. It will force her to be quiet for a few moments, at least.

(*Enter* KITTY ; *wears apron covered with flour.*)

KITTY. Just wait until you see my cake. It will make you die with envy.

HELEN. If we don't die from its heaviness, you may have all the glory. Do tell us how you made it ?

KITTY. First I sifted my flour.

FLORENCE (*touches her apron*). Yes, I should say that you did.

KITTY. I beat the yolks and whites of the eggs separately. Added sugar, salt, baking powder, and milk. I tell you, girls, it will melt in your mouth.

FLORENCE. Mab must write a sonnet upon your success.

(MABEL *runs on.*)

MABEL. What *is* the matter with your cake, Kitty ?

KITTY. Matter ? What do you mean ?

MABEL. It is running through the cracks of the oven door. It is melting.

KITTY. Oh, dear — it did look beautifully.

HELEN. Do you think that you forgot anything ?

MABEL. You have left the flour on the kitchen table.

KITTY. Some one catch me. (*Sinks into* FLORENCE'S *arms.*) I forgot the flour. (GIRLS *laugh.*)

MABEL. Alas ! poor Katherine ; to have your dreams of glory thus melt away !

KITTY. Mrs. Graham will never forgive me ; her floor will be a sight. Come, girls, and help me arrest the erratic wanderings of my emotional cake. (GIRLS *rush to door* R. *and exeunt except* FLORENCE ; *she reaches door as* POLLY *speaks.*)

POLLY. Do wait for me. (*Attempts to rise ; appears to be held by glue.*) Something holds me here.

FLORENCE. I should say so. That cheese-cloth has just been wet with glue. You are held fast, my pretty Polly.

POLLY. For mercy sakes, don't speak to me as though I were a parrot, Florence Baldwin! You will be offering me a cracker next. Do help me out of this.

FLORENCE. No, I think you had better take a little rest. (*Winds cheese-cloth about her ; covers her completely.*) Thus do I hold you prisoner. (*Runs off laughing.*)

POLLY. I call that mean. (*Tries to extricate herself.*) Well, I can take a nap anyway. (*Remains quiet.*)

(*Enter* MRS. GRAHAM.)

MRS. G. That kitchen floor is a sight. Cake dough from one door to another. I am afraid I shall regret having the sale here. My house and nerves will be worthy objects upon which to bestow this day's receipts. The stove looks dejected with so many failures. Something is burning. I can smell it. It is the candy. That will be ruined as well. (*Meets* HELEN *at door* R.) Helen, that candy will be spoiled.

HELEN. No, it won't. Sallie only tipped the kettle and lost half of it.

MRS. G. My house will be ruined.

HELEN. No, it won't, mother dear. (*Puts arm about her.*) Remember, it is for sweet charity. I have a secret to tell you.

MRS. G. A secret ?

HELEN (*puts finger to lips and looks cautiously about ; does not see* POLLY *who is hidden by the drapery*). I found a letter of Nan's the other day. It was from the school committee. (POLLY *stirs.*)

MRS. G. How do you know ?

HELEN. I overheard Nan telling Aunt Clarissa that she was expecting one. I have kept the letter.

MRS. G. (*catches her by arm*). Helen Graham! I am ashamed of you. You know better than to do such a thing. (POLLY *shows that she is listening.*)

HELEN. Wait, until I tell you. Unknown to us, Nan has passed the examinations and has received an appointment as teacher. A secret plotting going on beneath our very eyes. I intend to give the letter to Nan when it is too late for the appointment this year. She can try again next, but not until she has had time to learn that it is not wise to deceive those who have given her a home, food, and shelter.

MRS. G. I do not approve of this. You should have consulted me at once. If Nan wishes to teach school, I shall not stand in her way. I should be very glad to be free from supporting her.

HELEN. Yes, but what right has she to do such a thing without asking your consent ?

MRS. G. I should herald such good fortune with delight. Where is the letter ?

HELEN. In the pocket of the gown I wore on Wednesday.

MRS. G. Get it for me at once.

HELEN. I will after the sale is over. (*Takes her by arm.*) Come with me now and see how the candy is progressing.

MRS. G. But, Helen —

HELEN. I smell it burning. Come. (*Hurries* MRS. G. *out of room.*)

POLLY (*after making several unsuccessful attempts, unwinds the drapery*). Well, I never! A dynamite explosion is nothing in comparison to what I have heard. My sister Helen to do such a thing! It can't be possible. (*Finally succeeds in freeing herself from the table; rises.*) A novel way, I am sure, of being concealed to discover a secret. It is quite like a story. I will make it more so. A thrilling sequel. I will find the letter and tell Nan what Helen has done. There will be fireworks, and I will be in it. (*Makes for door* C.; *stops, comes down again.*) I don't know about that. If Helen has done wrong, it won't help matters to tell Nan of it. She is my sister, and I should shield her. That is my idea of a King's Daughter. I will make Nan think that I found it in my pocket after all. (*Exit* C.)

(*Enter* BETH HAMLIN *with vases and flowers, which she arranges upon flower table;* SALLIE *and* KITTY *bring in plates of candy.*)

SALLY. It is fortunate, Kitty, that we have had a generous donation of cake and candy. Your cake was a failure, and half of the candy served as a burnt offering upon the fire. (GIRLS *laugh.*)

(*Enter* MABEL *with numerous envelopes.*)

MABEL. There — a letter for each of us. They will serve as a blind to Miss Rebecca and the Deacon. (*Puts them in letter-box; at door* C.) Here comes Miss Rebecca now. Speak of the angels —

(*Enter* MISS REBECCA.)

REBECCA. Good-afternoon, girls. How is the good work progressing?

SALLIE. Finely. We only need your generous patronage to set the wheel in motion.

REBECCA (*at table* R.; *uses lorgnette*). How perfectly fascinating! Everything is in such perfect taste. I really shouldn't know which to choose.

KITTY. We can help you. (*Throws pink scarf around* MISS R.'S *neck.*) Pink is so becoming. It gives a peach-like glow to your delicate skin. (*Looks at* GIRLS, *who laugh behind* MISS R.'S *back.*)

REBECCA (*very much pleased*). Do you think so? My friends have always admired me in pink.

KITTY. I heard Deacon Starr say only the other day to my mother that if some people only knew how well they looked in pink, they would wear it always.

REBECCA. I will take this. How much?

KITTY. Two dollars.

REBECCA. Isn't that rather high?

KITTY (*with meaning*). Not when it is becoming, Miss Rebecca. (*Wraps scarf in paper.*)

SALLY (*draws* MISS REBECCA *to opposite table*). You must not be partial, Miss Rebecca. You will buy this comfortable pillow. (*Takes slumber pillow from table.*) It will be just the thing for your easy-chair.

REBECCA. I never use one. I always sit erect.

SALLIE. But how nice, when some one happens in for a cosey chat.

REBECCA. It is not necessary for any of my friends to make a lounging place of my sitting-room.

SALLIE. Not even the Deacon?

REBECCA (*hesitates*). Well, — I —

SALLIE. How becoming this would be to his beautiful iron gray hair! I can see the Deacon's curls resting upon it now.

REBECCA (*takes pillow quickly*). Where?

SALLIE (*laughing*). "In my mind's eye," Miss Rebecca. (GIRLS *laugh.*)

REBECCA. Oh, you silly girls! (*Sighs.*) I suppose I ought to buy it. Being a creature of impulse, I will. Where is your soda fountain?

(*Enter* FLORENCE.)

KITTY. You are just in time, Florence. Miss Rebecca is asking for the soda fountain. She still thirsts for something.

FLORENCE. The fountain is ready in the other room. (*Bows profoundly.*) Miss Rebecca, I shall be proud to draw for you the first glass of our refreshing beverage. (*Exeunt* MISS R. *and* FLORENCE.)

KITTY. This is too jolly for anything.

MABEL. We must try the post-office next. It grows wildly exciting. The plot thickens. (*Noise heard outside.*) What can be the matter?

(FLORENCE *and* MISS REBECCA *rush on followed by* HELEN ; *all laughing, their faces covered with foam.*)

FLORENCE. That was a surprise party.

HELEN (*at door* L.). Nan, bring a towel quick.

REBECCA. That is an entirely new way of taking soda — externally.

(*Enter* NAN *with towels ; helps them to remove the foam.*)

KITTY. How did it happen?

FLORENCE. I proceeded with flourishes and all sort of things to turn on the soda. Something gave way, — a screw, I guess, — and behold the result.

KITTY. Miss Rebecca can truly say, after you, the deluge.

(*Enter* RUTH.)

RUTH. Oh, girls! The soda is running away.

GIRLS. Oh, my! (*All exeunt.*)

REBECCA. Thank you, Nan. You always come to the rescue.

NAN. I do not think it has done any harm. Sorry that you lost your soda.

REBECCA. I can live without that. (*Looks cautiously about.*) Have you heard from the school committee?

NAN (*astonished*). How did you know that I expected to hear from them?

REBECCA. Deacon Starr told me that you had passed the examinations successfully.

NAN (*clasps her hands eagerly*). Then, I shall receive an appointment?

REBECCA. I don't know about that, but, being a creature of impulse, you know, I told the Deacon that if you didn't have one, I would never forgive him.

NAN (*takes* MISS R.'S *hand*). I can never thank you enough for your kindly interest.

(*Enter the* GIRLS.)

HELEN. Sorry, Miss Rebecca, but there isn't a drop of soda left. Mab, you might write some verses, not upon the flowing bowl, but the flowing soda.

MABEL. I will, and devote a few lines to Kitty's cake. That was flowing too. (GIRLS *laugh*.) Have you visited the post-office, Miss Rebecca?

REBECCA. No. Have you any mail for me?

KITTY (*at box*). Yes; here is one. It will cost you five cents to receive it.

REBECCA (*takes money from purse*). This fair will prove a mid-day robbery. (*Gives money to* KITTY, *who gives her letter;* GIRLS *watch her eagerly; she comes down to front of stage.*) I wonder from whom it can be. The handwriting is not familiar. Cannot imagine who wrote it. (*Sits in chair; looks at envelope;* GIRLS *show signs of impatience.*)

HELEN. Why don't you open it?

REBECCA. Oh, I often sit for hours wondering from whom it can be. (GIRLS *assume dejected air.*) The uncertainty is so delicious.

MABEL (*takes letter from box*). Here is one for Deacon Starr also. The handwriting looks like a woman's.

REBECCA (*aside*). Some unknown female writing to the Deacon? (*Tears open her letter;* GIRLS *watch her eagerly;* MISS R. *reads.*) Oh, I shall faint. The shock is too great for my nerves.

KITTY. Is it sorrow, Miss Rebecca?

REBECCA. Sorrow! (*With ecstasy.*) It is joy, my dear girl, joy.

KITTY. Do tell us, that we may share it with you.

REBECCA (*rises*). Share it with you? You know not what you ask. Be patient, and when you have reached *my* years of discre-

tion, this happiness may come to you. (GIRLS *convulsed; aside*.)
My impulse is to show this to the Deacon at once. No, I will first
see this fond lover. Ah, Romeo, that day in the woods, I did not
call your name in vain. (*Goes toward door* C.)

MABEL. This letter for the Deacon.

REBECCA. I will take it to him. (*Takes letter*.)

MABEL. Won't it be too much trouble?

REBECCA. Yes, it will be a trouble, but I am willing to sacrifice
myself. (*Aside*.) My heart is beating like an imprisoned bird.
Courage, Rebecca. (*Exit*.)

•KITTY. She has forgotten the pink scarf.

SALLIE. And the pillow. (*Both girls rush to door* C., *and call*
" *Miss Rebecca*.")

KITTY. She has gone. I must say that our little scheme for
bringing about a proposal from the Deacon will work mischief or a
happy result.

SALLIE. It is a pity we havn't more laggards in love to help in
the good cause. (*Arm about* RUTH.) Perhaps, we could help
Tom Mason a little.

RUTH. No, thank you, Sally. I can do all the helping that is
necessary in that direction.

KITTY. That is true, Ruth. The grass won't grow under your
feet.

RUTH (*makes deep courtesy*). Only long enough to make hay,
while the sun shines. (GIRLS *laugh*.)

HELEN. I am anxious about the success of the loan collection
we are to give this evening. Don't you think that we had better
rehearse the pictures?

KITTY. It will be such a bother to dress for them.

FLORENCE. Oh, no it won't. Let's do it.

KITTY. All right, and while we are dressing, Nan can get the
room ready.

(*Enter* POLLY.)

SALLIE. Hallo! Polly, where have you been?

POLLY. Looking for a letter, which I lost.

HELEN. Did you find it?

POLLY (*looks at* HELEN *with meaning*). Yes; some one had
taken it — by mistake.

HELEN. What do you mean, Polly Graham? (*Takes her by
arm*.)

POLLY (*throwing off* HELEN'S *hand*). Oh, nothing. (*Goes up
stage*.)

HELEN (*aside*). It can't be Nan's letter. No one knows where
it is.

FLORENCE. How did you like the arrangement for a seat, Polly?
You seemed to have a clinging fondness for it. (*Laughs*.)

POLLY. Yes, and I always shall. If you had not made me
prisoner, I never should have found —

FLORENCE. What?

POLLY. How — much I liked it.

HELEN. You two seem to be having all the fun to yourselves.

FLORENCE. Why, you remember when Polly threw herself down against the table, which was wet with glue.

HELEN. Yes.

FLORENCE. Well, when we all rushed out to help Kitty with her cake, Polly was left behind. Just for fun I wrapped her so completely in the cheese-cloth, that she might have listened to all the secrets (HELEN *starts*) in the world, without any one being the wiser.   .

HELEN (*aside to* POLLY). And you heard?

POLLY. Yes.

HELEN. Where is the letter?

POLLY. Out of your reach, my dear.

HELEN. Don't be silly, Polly. I only did it for fun.

POLLY. And I am only keeping it for fun.

HELEN. Nonsense! Come on, girls, we must get ready. Polly, will you find Nan and tell her to get the room ready for the pictures?

POLLY. Yes. (GIRLS *exeunt*.) Now, how shall I give that letter to Nan? (*Thinks a moment*.) I have it. (*Hands in pocket*.) A hole in my dress. (*Reaches down until hand touches hem of skirt*.) I will pretend I found it here. (*Slips letter in; goes up stage and looks out of window*.)

(*Enter* NAN *and* AUNT CLARISSA.)

AUNT C. It does seem strange that you have not heard. Have you seen Miss Grant?

NAN. Yes; and she is broken hearted. Her mother and the younger children depend upon her for support, and she will now be obliged to leave her home and seek a position elsewhere.

AUNT C. (*takes purse from pocket*). Let me give them something.

NAN. No indeed. That would not be right, when you have none to spare yourself.

AUNT C. You are right. (*Sits in chair; assumes an irritated air*.) You need not remind me of my poverty.

NAN. Oh, Aunt Clarissa! That is unkind. You know I would not do such a thing.

AUNT C. It is hard enough to be forced to live without money without being constantly reminded of it. (*Pretends to weep*.) It is dreadful to live with relatives who do not care for you.

NAN (*kneels beside her*). Don't cry, Aunt Clarissa. Perhaps the time will come when you can live with me. (AUNT C. *covers the side of face which is turned toward* NAN, *but shows to audience that she is listening intently and is pleased*.) Let me picture a new life for both of us. (*Soft music*.) If I secure my appointment as teacher, we will have a cosey home together. Just large enough for us. Oh, we must not forget Polly. She will always be welcome. In the summer, honeysuckle and wood-vine will twine itself about our door and we will have our supper in the garden. (*Arm about* AUNT C.) Won't that be lovely? Then in the winter, when I return from school, I will see your face at the window watching for me, and within a cheerful fire upon the hearth. You would be happy then, Aunt Clarissa?

AUNT C. Why would you do all this for me? I am cross and disagreeable, and can give you nothing in return.

NAN (*both rise*). Because you are alone in the world, as I am. I don't think that you are cross at heart; your trouble has made you so. As for giving me anything, only love me and I will ask no other reward.

AUNT C. Don't talk of this any more. I am tired.

POLLY (*comes down*). Hallo, Nan! I have been looking for you. The girls wish to rehearse for the pictures, and would like to have you get the room ready.

NAN. Certainly. Aunt Clarissa shall see them. (*Places chair down extreme R. of stage.*)

POLLY. Yes, she shall be audience. (AUNT C. *sits in chair; wire should be drawn above half-way up the stage, upon which are curtains, which until needed are drawn closely back at side of stage.* NAN *and* POLLY *bring from R. entrance a draped easel, upon which is large gilt frame. During this* POLLY *is very nervous and makes several attempts to speak.*)

NAN. Why, Polly! How nervous you are! What is the matter?

POLLY. Oh, nothing. (*Puts hand in pocket.*) Dear me! I always have a rip in my dress.

NAN (*laughing*). I am afraid you do.

POLLY. I expect I shall find a long lost treasure, sometime.

NAN (*kneeling beside her and feeling of hem of skirt*). It will be as wonderful as Pandora's box. Why, here is something. It feels like a letter. Oh, Polly, perhaps —

POLLY (*takes letter out*). It is. Well, I never!

NAN (*taking it*). It has been opened.

POLLY. Has it? Oh, I remember. I noticed when they gave it to me at the post-office that it was not closely sealed. Rubbing against my pocket must have unfastened it.

NAN (*who has been reading letter*). Aunt Clarissa, let me read this to you. (*Reads.*) "Dear Miss Graham : I am pleased to inform you that we have an appointment for you as teacher." (*Speaks.*) Isn't that too lovely for anything ? Now, Aunt Clarissa, we will have that cottage.

POLLY. What cottage?

NAN. The one that Aunt Clarissa and I are to have.

POLLY. If you have a cottage, I shall be "in it."

NAN. I should hope so. (*Reads.*) "We will give you the position filled by Miss Grant." (*Dazed, puts hand to her head.*) I don't understand.

POLLY. I do. Just because Deacon Starr is interested in Miss
Rebecca and she likes you, he has persuaded the committee to give
you Miss Grant's class.

NAN. But I could never take it from her; and yet — it means
so much to me.

AUNT C. Why should you sacrifice yourself for Miss Grant?
She is nothing to you.

NAN. She has more at stake than I have; the support of her
mother and sisters. I only lose my freedom and independence.

AUNT C. Think, Nan, how much that means to you.

NAN. Don't tempt me, Aunt Clarissa. It has been my dream,
waking and sleeping. What shall I do?

POLLY. You might speak to the school committee.

NAN. I will write to them at once. (*Writes at small table back
of stage.*)

AUNT C. (*aside*). This will be a test of her strength and courage.
Will she disappoint me?

(*Enter* MISS REBECCA.)

REBECCA. I am all excitement. I do believe that the Deacon
is jealous. I watched him read his letter and heard him say —
"Some one in love with my Rebecca." Who knows, after these
weary years of waiting —

POLLY. You forgot something. (*Gives parcels to her.*)

REBECCA. Yes, I came back for them. (*Laughs embarrassedly.*)
I thought that the Deacon might call this evening, and, if so, he
would enjoy resting his head upon this lovely cushion.

POLLY. And shall you wear the pink scarf, Miss Rebecca?

REBECCA (*taps her playfully with lorgnette*). Oh, you silly
child!

NAN (*comes down*). I have written to Deacon Starr. Miss
Rebecca, will you do me a favor? You know the Deacon so
well.

REBECCA. Yes, I suppose I do.

NAN. He has given me Miss Grant's position. Won't you ask
him to give me another?

REBECCA. Yes, I will; but you know school committees do
not like to change their decisions.

NAN. But you have so much influence with him.

REBECCA (*laughs coquettishly*). Well, I will try. (*Aside.*)
I wonder if my Romeo hovers near. (*Exit.*)

AUNT C. And if they refuse to make this change?

NAN. I dare not think of what would be my duty. (*Stands
leaning against door* C.; *rests head upon arm; Enter* HELEN, SAL-
LIE, *and* FLORENCE *from* L., MRS. GRAHAM *from* R.)

SALLIE. You are just in time, Mrs. Graham; we are to rehearse
the pictures.

MRS. G. I shall expect a reserved seat in the orchestra.

HELEN. And you shall have it. (*Places chair extreme* L. *of stage ; both* MRS. G, *and* AUNT C. *have needle-work or knitting.*) Now, Nan, you may arrange the curtains. (NAN *comes down and draws curtains in front of easel ; she stands at one side and draws curtains as pictures are ready.* HELEN *stands by* MRS. G. *and announces them.*)
HELEN. All ready?
KITTY (*from behind curtain*). Yes.

(*Give six representations; the* GIRLS *each dressed to represent some well-known picture. Each one stands behind the frame in turn and the curtains are only drawn to the sides of the frame. All the* GIRLS *should be ready so that one can follow the other without waits. Soft music. After the sixth,* FLORENCE *puts her head out between the curtains. If difficult to do on account of change of costume, extra girls can be introduced for the pictures.*)

FLORENCE. Wait a moment. We have two more; perfect gems of art.
HELEN. Hurry, then. Our audience will get tired.
AUNT C. I could look at pictures all night.
MRS. G. So could I. The fair will prove a success.

(SALLIE *enters from behind curtain with Kodak.*)

SALLIE. I don't mean to lose these.
FLORENCE (*inside*). Don't laugh, Kitty. Ready. (NAN *draws curtains ; discloses* KITTY *in frame, her face and apron covered with flour.*)
FLORENCE. The flour [Flower] of the family.
HELEN (*applauds*). Good! You put so much flour on yourself, Kitty, you will soon be the staff of life for your family. (KITTY *laughs ;* NAN *draws curtains after* SALLIE *snaps Kodak.*)
SALLIE. We ought to have the Deacon and Miss Rebecca in the picture together; we could call it "At last."
FLORENCE. Ready. (NAN *draws curtain ;* POLLY *is discovered behind frame covered as before with black paint.*) Our artist.
(*All applaud ;* SALLIE *takes picture ;* NAN *draws curtain to side of stage ; the* GIRLS *help to remove easel.*)
FLORENCE. Don't think that we will give the last two to the promiscuous public; they might not appreciate them. (GIRLS *exeunt except* NAN *and* POLLY.)

(*Enter* MISS REBECCA.)

REBECCA. A note for you, Miss Nan.
NAN (*takes it eagerly*). From the Deacon?
REBECCA. Yes.
NAN (*reads note*). What shall I do? There is no other position. The Deacon says that if I wish, I can give mine to Miss

Grant. Oh, I can't do that. (*Hesitates;* Aunt C. *watches her.*) I will.

Rebecca. Keep it yourself. Let Miss Grant take care of herself.

Nan. No, it would not be right. I appreciate your kindness and that of Deacon Starr, but I cannot take the bread and butter from her family. (*Writes at table.*)

Mrs. G. What is all this about ? (Helen *enters.*)

Polly. The school committee have given Miss Grant's position to Nan.

Mrs. G. I do not see why there should be so much talk about it. It will be a very easy thing to accept.

Nan (*comes down with note*). But I cannot.

Mrs. G. Cannot! Why not, pray ?

Nan.' I would be taking away the only support of the Grant family. It would cause a separation. As for me, I will wait another year.

Mrs. G. Indeed! You will do nothing of the kind. I have supported you, given you a home all these years, and now that you have an opportunity of lifting the burden from my shoulders and taking care of yourself, you throw it aside, as though it were of no consequence.

Nan. I do appreciate all you have done for me, Aunt Graham, and regret that I must still be a burden to you. I had hoped that, by making myself useful, I had in a measure repaid your kindness.

Polly. And so you have, Nan. You have done everything for us. (*Crosses to her.*)

Nan. I will not take the position from Miss Grant. (*Holds out letter to* Miss Rebecca.) Here is my answer, Miss Rebecca.

Helen (*steps forward and takes letter; holds it behind her*). You show your gratitude in a wonderful way.

Nan (*excited*). Be careful what you say, Helen Graham. You have thought because I was poor and dependent upon your mother's bounty, that I had no hopes, no ambitions beyond the privilege of answering to your beck and call. I have borne your taunts and slurs with submission. I will, no longer. Give me that letter. (Polly *leaves her and stands behind* Helen.)

Helen. No, I will not. I cannot aid you in taking such a foolish step.

Polly (*snatches letter*). But I will. (*Gives it to* Miss Rebecca.)

Helen. Polly, give me that letter.

Polly. Excuse me, Helen. It isn't mine to give.

Rebecca. You shall have an answer at once. You have always been kind to me, Miss Nan.. (*Holds out hand, which* Nan *takes.*) If you need a friend, I am yours to command. (*Exit.*)

Aunt C. Nan, leave us for a few moments. I wish to see your aunt alone. (Nan *and* Polly *exeunt.*)

Helen. Am I included in this private interview?

Aunt C. You are not. I wish to speak with your mother.

HELEN (*with sarcasm; makes mock courtesy*). I am sure my mother appreciates the honor. (*Exit laughing.*)

AUNT C. Eleanor Graham, how have you brought up your daughter? why have you allowed her to sneer at those who have less of these worldly goods than herself?

MRS. G. Was it for the purpose of criticising me that you have requested this interview? If so, you must excuse me, as my time is valuable.

AUNT C. I wish to speak of Nan. Does it ever occur to you that it might have been *your* daughter who had been left to the care and charity of her relatives? Are you treating Nan as you would wish *your* daughter to be done by?

MRS. G. She has had a home, plenty to eat and to wear. What more would you expect of me?

AUNT C. Enough love and thoughtful care, that her one thought and ambition would not be to leave the roof that has sheltered her. Young girls meet here, — call themselves " The King's Daughters." Their mission is to do good. Helen sews for the poor, gives food to the hungry "in His name," yet beneath your own roof you permit one to live a life of starvation.

MRS. G. (*rises*). "Starvation!" You use rather strong words, Aunt Clarissa.

AUNT C. (*rises*). Because I mean them. You let Nan starve: her heart go hungry for love and affection. Helen treats her shamefully, yet she calls herself a King's Daughter. Let Nan do as she will with this appointment; she has no money with which to help the needy, yet permit her to make this sacrifice, which would mean more to her than the giving of money would to you.

MRS. G. I will do nothing of the kind. She shall not throw aside such an opportunity. She will recognize my authority.

AUNT C. Have a care, Eleanor Graham ; mark what I say. If you persist in this tyranny, the time will come when you will regret it with your whole heart.

MRS. G. You seem to take a great interest in this niece of ours. It is a pity you cannot bequeath to her a fortune.

AUNT C. (*at door* C.). It is a pity; but she shall have all that is mine to give — love and devotion. (*Exit.*)

MRS. G. (*laughing*). What a stir over a small matter! I only wish my authority to be obeyed. Nan must not think that she can have her own way in such a matter. I will help the Grants. There is no need of making a tragedy of this. To hear Aunt Clarissa, one would think that I was committing some crime. (*Exit.*)

(*Enter* GIRLS.)

KITTY. Only one hour more and the doors will be open to the surging populace without.

FLORENCE. Did Polly finish her artistic effort?

KITTY. Not quite. The paint gave out. She put too much on her face and hands.

FLORENCE. She must have true genius, then. Where is Sallie? She was to take our picture.

(*Enter* SALLIE *with Kodak.*)

SALLIE. Who calls?

KITTY. We await your coming, fair maiden. We would have you immortalize our beautiful features.

SALLIE. All right; group yourselves together.

KITTY. We couldn't very well group ourselves apart, could we?

SALLIE. Kittie, if you are so brilliant, the atmosphere around you will be too dazzling, and you will spoil the picture.

(*Enter* POLLY.)

POLLY. Oh, wait for me.

SALLIE. Come on, my cherub. There is always room for you.
(GIRLS *form in group at back of stage;* SALLIE *arranges them.*)

SALLIE. Beth, stop giggling. Ruth, don't have that tragic air.

KITTY. She is thinking of Tom. (*Sighs.*) Wish I had a Tom.

SALLIE. You won't even have a picture, if you don't stop talking.

KITTY. I am mum, only I am so hungry.

FLORENCE. Would you like a piece of cake, Kitty? (GIRLS *laugh.*)

KITTY (*groans*). Don't speak of cake to me.

SALLIE. Don't move. Steady. (*Snaps Kodak.*) There! It won't be good for anything. Kitty was one vast smile.

KITTY. Try again. I will promise you I will keep sober.

SALLIE. No, can't waste any more time upon you. Here comes Miss Rebecca. She seems to have a hovering fondness for us.

MABEL. "Hovering fondness" is good. Where did you get it, Sallie?

SALLIE (*taps forehead*). From the rich quarries of my brain.

MABEL. Goodness, Sallie! Your "rich quarries" and my slumbering genius would make a fine combination. Oh, you were to read our palms.

(*Enter* MISS REBECCA.)

REBECCA. Where is Nan?

POLLY. She will be here in a moment. Come and have your fortune told.

REBECCA. I do not need to have my fortune told from my hand.

SALLIE (*takes her hand;* GIRLS *grouped about them*). The fate line has been broken. Once, twice, — ah, Miss Rebecca, I fear you have been a wicked flirt.

REBECCA (*sighs*). Yes, a new love has come constantly into my life.

SALLIE. But in the end the old love will triumph.
REBECCA (*eagerly*). The Deacon?
SALLIE. Yes. A laggard in love; yet the time will come when, like the brave Lochinvar,
MABEL. He will give —

> "One touch to her hand, and one word in her ear,
> When they reached the hall door, and the charger stood near.
> So light to the croupe the fair lady he swung,
> So light to the saddle before her he sprung.
> 'She is won! we are gone! over bank, bush and scaur;
> They'll have fleet steeds that follow' quoth" *old* DEACON STARR.

(GIRLS *laugh*.)

KITTY. Think of old Deacon Starr, a gay Lothario.
REBECCA (*indignantly*). "Old" Deacon Starr indeed! His hair may be gray, his step slower than in his youthful days, but his heart beats as warmly as that of Tom Mason or any other silly boy lover. (*Goes up stage.*)
KITTY. Ha, ha! Our love affair is progressing finely. It only needs one of your pot-boilers, Mab, to light the flame.

(*Enter* RUTH *wearing* NAN's *old-fashioned bonnet.*)

RUTH. See what I have found. This old-fashioned bonnet.
POLLY (*takes it from her head*). Which you will please take off, Miss Ruth. That belongs to Nan.
RUTH. You needn't be so snappy, Polly Graham. It is too old to hurt.
HELEN. Didn't you ever hear about Nan's legacy?
FLORENCE. Never knew she had one.
HELEN (*takes bonnet from* POLLY *and holds it up*). Here it is.
KITTY. She couldn't live upon the income of that very long. Why does she think so much of it?
POLLY. Because it was a gift of love, and Nan does not have many of those.
HELEN. I should prefer a more substantial gift of love than this old bonnet.

(*Enter* MRS. GRAHAM *and* NAN.)

MRS. G. You are still obstinate?
NAN. If you wish to call it that.
MRS. G. And you value my authority as nothing. Do you think it right after all these years that I have given you a home?

(*Enter* AUNT CLARISSA.)

NAN. Don't make it so hard for me, Aunt Graham. Even for all your kindness, I cannot do this act of injustice.
MRS. G. Then there is but one thing for you to do. You must leave this house.

NAN. Aunt Graham !

AUNT C. Eleanor, you surely do not mean that.

MRS. G. I do. My house is no longer her home, if she refuses to obey me. (GIRLS *group together ; express wonderment.*)

HELEN (*crosses to her mother*). Mother, are you in earnest ?

MRS. G. Yes ; I wish to teach her a lesson.

HELEN. You had better think twice, Nan. You do not know what it is to be without a home.

NAN. I have had a roof to shelter me, clothes to wear, food, but the true atmosphere of home, — love and affection, — I have never known. I am able to work ; money will bring me all that I have had.

HELEN. Who will give you the love and affection?

AUNT C. (*crosses to* NAN ; *arm about her*). I will.

MRS. G. Don't be foolish, Aunt Clarissa.

AUNT C. You would turn this child from your doors ?

MRS. G. She must be punished for her obstinacy and disobedience. But this is nonsense. I will do nothing hasty. We will leave you alone to think this over, Nan ; perhaps a few moments of quiet will bring you to your senses. (*All exeunt, leaving* NAN *alone.*)

NAN. And this is the end of all my dreams. Banished from the only home I have ever known, and only because I will not take from another.

(*Enter* POLLY.)

⌐ POLLY. Don't you give in, Nan. I will go with you, and we can live together.

NAN. No, Polly dear. The wide world is no place for you. (*Arm around her.*) Stay where you are, and think of me and love me. When the way is rough and my journey hard, to know that you are safe and happy, loving me, will be an oasis in the great wide desert. (*Takes up old-fashioned bonnet, which is upon table* L. ; *kisses it.*) You little thought, Uncle John, when you left me this legacy how much I should need a shelter, after all. (*Sinks upon her knees, sobbing by table ;* POLLY *wipes her eyes and goes up stage to window.*)

(*Enter* AUNT CLARISSA ; *crosses to* NAN *and lays her hand upon her shoulder.*)

AUNT C. Nan.

NAN. Oh, Aunt Clarissa!

AUNT C. Would it not be better, Nan, to obey your aunt ?

NAN (*turns and looks at* AUNT C.). And you ask me that, Aunt Clarissa ?

AUNT C. Then you are determined?

NAN. Yes. I will do as I think right for all the aunt Grahams in the world. (*Sadly ; turns to* AUNT C.) But where shall I go ?

AUNT C. (*sits in chair down* R. *and draws* NAN *to her, who kneels*). Listen. Do you remember the picture of a home which you painted for me?

NAN. Yes; but it will prove only a castle in the air.

AUNT C. Which I propose to turn into a little cottage in this very town.

NAN (*clasps her hands eagerly*). Oh, if you only could!

AUNT C. It will be very small, and we must work hard. Will you share it with me?

NAN. Share it with you? (*Arm about* AUNT C.; *kisses her.*) Oh, that would be too good to be true.

AUNT C. (*both rise*). Be true to your convictions, my dear, and I will help you.

NAN. You have made me as strong as iron. I have heart to do anything now.

(*Enter* MRS. G. *and* HELEN.)

MRS. G. I hope you have decided wisely, Nan.

NAN (*quietly*). I have.

MRS. G. What will you do?

NAN. I leave here at once.

AUNT C. And I go with her.

MRS. G. Then go, both of you, and learn a lesson from your obstinacy.

POLLY (*throws arms about* NAN). Oh, Nan, you will not leave me?

MRS. G. Polly, come here.

NAN (*takes* POLLY'S *arms away*). Your mother is speaking, Polly. (*Kisses her.*) Good-bye, dear.

HELEN. And what do you expect to gain from this sacrifice?

NAN (*arm about* AUNT CLARISSA; *both at door* C.). Gain? Only the consciousness of well-doing; for that which I have done has not been for what the world may say of it, but " In His Name."

(*Tableau* : NAN *standing at entrance* C., *one arm around* AUNT CLARISSA, *the other, upon which bonnet is hanging, raised, hand pointing upward;* POLLY *leaning against table* L., *sobbing;* MRS. G. *and* HELEN *at* R., *looking at* NAN.)

QUICK CURTAIN.

ACT III.

"THE FAIRY GODMOTHER."

SCENE. — *A hay-field. Drop of country scene at back of stage. Trees* R. *and* L. ; *down extreme* R. *and* L. *on either side, a mound of hay.* RUTH *asleep on mound at* R. ; MABEL *writing on mound at* L. ; KITTY, FLORENCE, SALLIE, *and* BETH *raking hay. All wear milking-maid's costumes. As curtain is raised,* GIRLS *are laughing and throwing hay at one another.*

KITTY (*throws down rake*). It is very romantic to read of :

> " Maud Muller, on a summer's day,
> Raked the meadow, sweet with hay,"

but the realization of it is rather warm, and the romance of it vanishes into thin air. (*Sits upon mound* L. ; *fans herself with hat.*) My blood is boiling.

SALLIE. Then, for mercy's sake, do come away from that mound of hay. With your blood at boiling-point, and Mab's genius burning, we shall have a conflagration. (GIRLS *rake hay to either side of stage, leaving* C. *clear.*)

KITTY. What are you writing, Mab?

MABEL. My first love-story.

GIRLS (*throw down rakes and rush to mound*). Oh, do read it to us !

MABEL. It isn't finished yet. I tell you, girls, it is a great responsibility to dispose of one's hero and heroine satisfactorily.

FLORENCE. To hear you talk in that cold-blooded fashion, one would think that these creatures of your imagination were inanimate objects, to be hermetically sealed, labelled, and dismissed when called for.

MABEL. I am just at the point where it would be necessary to label them " Handle with care." I don't know whether to have the hero fall in love with the heroine, or to let him die.

GIRLS. Oh, no !

KITTY. That would be mean. How would you like to have a man die ?

MABEL. It would depend upon the man. There are some who shine better as *dead* heroes. (*Reflects.*) Yes, I think that I will let him live.

FLORENCE. Noble girl. How happy you will make the heroine. Read it to us.

MABEL. No, it isn't ready. Let us talk of this beautiful day,

SALLIE. It seems quite like a romance.

KITTY. An unknown person becomes owner of Grafton Manse, invites The King's Daughters to spend the entire day upon her estates, and will not show herself until the ball this evening. We were requested to dress in dairy-maids' costumes and here we are. Hay-making at three; visit the dairy at four; a feast of good things out here beneath the trees; a ball in the evening, and that ends the programme.

BETH. And we haven't an idea who our hostess is; whether she is young or old. I think that it is the same one who has been giving us money to use amongst the poor.

FLORENCE. Whoever it may be, she is doing good for the love of it and not for ostentation. (*Rises.*) I say, God bless our hostess!

(*Enter* AUNT CLARISSA *with basket.*)

KITTY. Yes, and so say I. When we do know her, if we don't express our thanks, it will be because we have lost the power of speech.

AUNT C. There is gratitude in your hearts for some one?

GIRLS (*rise*). Aunt Clarissa?

FLORENCE. We were speaking of our new neighbor, the owner of Grafton Manse. She must be very happy, doing so much good.

AUNT C. She must be very fond of young people, don't you think so?

KITTY. She will make the young people very fond of her. Won't you sit down and rest?

AUNT C. It is Nan's birthday, and I must be at home when she returns from her work.

KITTY. Let me carry your basket for you. It must be heavy. (*Takes basket.*)

AUNT C. The King's Daughters have been very kind to me. I wish I could do something for you all in return.

FLORENCE. You do. Every day some one of our poor is helped. You may not have money to give, but think how many are made happy in that little cottage of yours. You never turn any one away hungry from your doors. Of course you are going to the Manse to-night to see the ball?

AUNT C. Dear me, no. What would a poor old lady like myself be doing at a ball. I will leave that for the younger ones. I would like to have Nan go.

KITTY. And so she shall. I will lend her one of my party gowns.

SALLIE. Yes; and she shall have my loveliest fan.

AUNT C. You are all very kind. I will try to persuade her. (AUNT C. *and* KITTY *go up stage.*)

FLORENCE. Good-by, Aunt Clarissa; don't forget the ball.

BETH. And you shall have one of my prettiest gowns. (AUNT CLARISSA *and* KITTY *exeunt.*)

MABEL. Only think of Aunt Clarissa and Nan living together

in the little cottage at the end of the town. Nan is working hard
for Miss Long the milliner, and she seems as happy as a queen.
Where is Helen?

SALLIE. She has deserted us since Nan left the Grahams.
Helen has not been the same girl. Something is troubling her.

(*Enter* POLLY ; *she has two roses in her hand.*)

BETH. Where is Polly?

POLLY (*jumps upon mound* R. *slides down, waking* RUTH).
Here I am.

RUTH (*jumping up*). Heavens! What was that ? A land-
slide.

POLLY. No, my dear. A girl slide.

RUTH. You spoiled a beautiful dream. It was about —

GIRLS. Tom ?

RUTH. No, you sillies. It was our unknown benefactress. I
thought she proved to be some one whom we had always known.

KITTY. Dreams go by contraries. That wouldn't be possible.
In this small town, a mouse couldn't stir, much less a woman, without the entire population being made aware of it. Who is to be
favored with your flowers, Polly?

POLLY. Nan, of course. It is her birthday. I am on the road
to her house now.

MABEL. Are you? I thought it was a hay-mound.

POLLY. Don't let any of that brilliancy escape, Mab ; you need
it all for your pot-boilers.

RUTH. May we go with you?

POLLY. Yes, only the one that gets there last, must make the ·
presentation speech.

FLORENCE. I won't lose a moment. You don't catch me speech-
making. (*Makes for back of stage ;* GIRLS *follow her.*)

POLLY. Come back. That isn't fair. We must all start together. (GIRLS *return and stand in a line.*) Now, one, two,
three, *go.* (GIRLS *rush off laughing ;* POLLY *runs with them to
back of stage, then stops.*) They can have the *run,* and I will have
the *fun* of making the speech. I was awake all night thinking of
it. I don't intend that my eloquence shall be nipped in the bud.
(*Exit leisurely.*)

(*Enter* MISS REBECCA, L., *in pink costume ; carries pink parasol.*)

REBECCA. The very air breathes mystery and romance. As I
wander beneath the trees whose rustling leaves bid me a silvery
welcome, I dare not give utterance to my thoughts for fear he is
hovering near. Aroused by the pangs of jealousy, the Deacon
has all but spoken ; yet I withhold the one bit of encouragement
that he is waiting for, hoping that my fond and mysterious lover,
who calls himself my " Romeo," may come to me. A sweet delicious uncertainty. A fortunate woman you are indeed, Rebecca.

Two lovers who wait, each eager to call me his. Often my fancy leads me to picture myself coming unawares upon my would-be hero. (*Crosses stage ; sees pair of boots and man's hat on* R. *side of mound* R. *half hidden by the hay ; screams.*) What do I see? A pair of boots and a man's hat. It is he, — my Romeo.

(*Enter* FLORENCE *and* SALLIE *running.*)

FLORENCE. .What is the matter? We heard you scream.
SALLIE. What is it, Miss Rebecca?
REBECCA (*agitated*). Oh, nothing. I thought that I saw some one.
FLORENCE. Where?
REBECCA (*points*). There, in the hay. (GIRLS *look.*)
SALLIE. A man's hat and boots peering forth. If Mab were only here she could weave a romance. She would probably condemn this man to be one of her dead heroes.
REBECCA. I was so frightened; my heart is in a flutter. (*Sinks upon mound* L.)
FLORENCE (*to* SALLIE). We do not need Mab to romance for us. Let's have some fun.
SALLIE. I havn't an idea how, but go ahead.
FLORENCE. Have you heard the rumor, Miss Rebecca, that a strange man has been seen about town? (MISS REBECCA *starts ;* FLORENCE *looks at* SALLIE, *who nods that she understands.*)
SALLIE. Yes, they say that he is in love with some one.
FLORENCE. Wouldn't it be great fun if we should discover that beneath this hat is the noble alabaster brow of the man whose coming is so mysterious.
REBECCA (*rises*). I beg you will not disturb the man whoever he may be. He is evidently very tired. It would be cruel to awaken him.
FLORENCE. Yet, by so doing, we might learn who is the fair object for which his heart yearns. It might be you, Miss Rebecca.
REBECCA (*coquettishly*). Oh, no.
SALLIE (*with dignity*). It might be Sallie Browning.
REBECCA. Oh, no. (*Corrects herself.*) Oh, yes.
FLORENCE. Whether Miss Rebecca, Sallie Browning or Florence Baldwin, I intend to arouse the slumbering hero. (*Crosses to* R.)
REBECCA. Don't, Miss Kitty. If it should be he, it might be embarrassing to find three here.
FLORENCE. Very well, you go, Miss Rebecca.
REBECCA. I could not think of leaving you alone here. I will remain.
FLORENCE. We will protect one another. There is safety in numbers, you know. What would Deacon Starr say if he should happen by and saw you kneeling before the prostrate form of an unknown man. His courage would slip away.
SALLIE (*at back of stage*). There goes the Deacon now in the

direction of your house. What a pity to have him disappointed in his call.

REBECCA. I will go. (*Makes for back of stage.*)

FLORENCE (*who is at mound* R. *looking at hat and boots*). Our hero stirs.

REBECCA (*comes down again*). I will stay.

SALLIE (*looking off*). Some one is speaking to the Deacon — the fascinating Miss Brett.

REBECCA (*makes for back of stage again*). I will go.

FLORENCE (*same business as before*). He smiles in his sleep. He is dreaming of her.

REBECCA (*comes down again; hesitates; makes for back of stage again*). I know not which way to turn.

FLORENCE (*goes to her*). Go, Miss Rebecca, and if you prove to be the one, I will come to you at once. Poor man; the uncertainty of his fate has made him weary. You would treat him kindly.

REBECCA (*takes* FLORENCE'S *hand; wipes eyes*). I will, I promise you. My heart has always a tender spot for lonely people. (*Exit* L.)

FLORENCE. Ha, ha. That is the best joke yet. The girls will just howl when they hear of it. (*Sinks laughing upon mound.*)

SALLIE (*sitting beside her*). I laugh with you, Florence, but I don't see the point.

FLORENCE (*rises and crosses to mound,* R.). Wait until I show you. (*Holds up hat and boots.*) The Alpha and Omega of Romeo. Ha, ha.

SALLIE. And you knew this all the time?

FLORENCE. Of course I did. The hat that hides from view the noble alabaster brow. Ha, ha; what shall we do with these?

SALLIE. To whom do they belong?

FLORENCE. To old Tom, the gardener. We will hang them upon this tree. (*Hangs them on tree at* R.) And we will write a note. (*Takes pencil and paper from pocket.*)

SALLIE. Write something short and sweet.

FLORENCE (*writes*). There! We lead the club on match-making. (*Puts paper in pocket of coat.*) Now to find the girls and tell the joke.

SALLIE. Yes, and I must have my Kodak for the final tableau. (*Exeunt* R.)

(*Enter* NAN, L.)

NAN. What a glorious day for the hay-makers. (*Takes hay and smells of it.*) New-mown hay — how sweet and refreshing. (*Sinks upon mound.*) I can hardly realize that I am the same Nan Graham who lived a month ago. The sun seems to shine brighter, the earth looks lovelier to me, and all because I am happy. It is the old story of Cinderella and her fairy godmother. Aunt Clarissa does not send me to balls in a coach and four; no glass slipper to lead the way to a royal husband ; but with her love and kindness, she has transformed my life from one of drudgery to one of peace and contentment. (*Rises.*) To-day I can breathe the sweetness of the air, and feel that it is good to be alive. (*Walks to back of stage.*)

(*Enter* GIRLS, *followed by* POLLY.)

KITTY. Here is Nan, now.

NAN. Were you looking for me?

KITTY. Yes, we have been to your house to wish you many returns of the day.

NAN. How kind of you.

POLLY. I brought you these flowers from my garden.

MABEL. A speech, Polly. You were last.

POLLY. Oh, I don't know how.

KITTY. Yes, you do. (GIRLS *lead her to mound of hay at* L., *and help her to mount.*)

POLLY. I can't make a speech. I will paint one. (GIRLS *laugh.*)

BETH. That would be too expensive, Polly. You used all the black paint Mr. Gray had in his store.

POLLY. If Kitty will present Nan with a cake, I will. (GIRLS *laugh.*)

RUTH. Yes, and our local reporter will have an account of it in the weekly *Argus*. " The presentation of the cake so affected the recipient, that she melted into tears." (GIRLS *laugh.*)

KITTY (*throws handful of hay at* POLLY). Pauline, you are treading upon dangerous ground. Come, make your prettiest bow, my dear.

POLLY (*makes bow ; stumbles and slides from mound ;* GIRLS *laugh*). I wasn't born for lofty heights. Roses one, roses two, these, dear Nan, I picked for you. (*Gives roses to* NAN ; GIRLS *applaud.*)

NAN (*takes them and throws arm around* POLLY). Thank you, little sweetheart. (*Kisses her.*) Your roses are just like yourself— fresh and pure ; and your speech, what I like best.

KITTY. It is time to visit the dairy ; come on, girls.

BETH. All right; come, Polly.

POLLY. No, thank you ; I prefer to stay with Nan.

RUTH. Of course we mean for Nan to come.

NAN. It is ever so kind of you, girls, but Aunt Clarissa will be waiting for me.

KITTY. All right. (GIRLS *exeunt.*)

NAN (*both seated upon mound*). Now we can have a cosey chat all by ourselves. (*Smells of roses.*) You never forgot me, Polly.

POLLY. How could I? It is so lonely without you at home, Nan. I wish you were back again.

NAN (*arm about* POLLY). No, you don't, Polly, dear.

POLLY. Not for your sake, but for my own. I know that you are happier with Aunt Clarissa, but you work so hard.

NAN. I don't mind it. It is so lovely to work for some one who gives you more than money in return — *love*. Aunt Clarissa is so good to me.

POLLY. She seemed so cross when she was at our house, and now she is so pleasant and lovely. Something is the matter with Helen, Nan. She never scolds me now. I think that she is sorry for treating you so badly.

NAN (*rises*). Oh, no, I can't think that. She has never been to see me. (*Bitterly.*) I might have starved, and she would not have lifted a finger to help me. Never mind, Polly, dear, I did not starve, and am happier than I have ever been in all my life. The Grant family are content, and when I see their grateful faces, I feel thankful that it was in my power to help them.

(*Enter* MRS. GRAHAM.)

MRS. G. Polly.

NAN (*turns and sees her*). Aunt Graham?

MRS. G. This is the first time that we have meet, Nan, since you left my house. Are you not tired of your wilfulness and the hard work?

NAN. I am not tired of the love and affection which Aunt Clarissa bestows upon me.

MRS. G. I did not intend to drive you from my doors; I only wished to be obeyed.

NAN. You did me a kindness then, more than any of us realized. I would not give up this freedom, the knowledge that I am no longer a dependent, for all the world.

MRS G. Will you make your home with us again? I am sorry for what I did.

NAN (*goes to her and takes her hand*). Thank you, Aunt Graham. I appreciate how hard this must be for you, but I could never again place myself under Helen's tyranny.

MRS. G. And if she, too, asked you to come?

(*Enter* AUNT CLARISSA.)

NAN (*arm about* AUNT C.). Not if she asked me a thousand times, would I leave Aunt Clarissa. She has been father and mother to me.

AUNT C. What are you asking of Nan, Eleanor?

MRS. G. To call my home hers again.

NAN (*takes* AUNT CLARISSA'S *face in both hands; looks at her a moment; kisses her*). Do you need an answer? (NAN *crosses to* POLLY; AUNT C. *to* MRS. GRAHAM.)

AUNT C. You see, we are both happy and contented, Eleanor. Your measure was a harsh one, but the sorrow of that day has been wiped out a hundred fold by the peacefulness and happiness of our lives. Unwittingly, you gave to me the love of a girl's heart which had been hungry so long. I came into her life when she needed me most, and the wealth of her affection is mine. You may think of me as poor, but no richer legacy can come to a woman than the love which I now possess.

MRS. G. (*sinks upon mound at* R; *weeps*). Then there is no atonement that I can make?

AUNT C. (*hand upon* MRS. G's *shoulder*). Eleanor, when the time comes, that your daughter Helen has learned the true meaning of "A King's Daughter," I will forgive and forget all.

MRS. G. She has learned that already. She has not known one happy moment, since Nan left us.

AUNT C. So much the better. Her lesson must be a severe one. (*Offers hand to* MRS. G.) Never forget again that when a child is placed under your protection and care, it means that love goes with it. Come, Nan.

NAN. Yes, Aunt Clarissa. (*Crosses to her.*) I shall expect you soon, Polly.

AUNT C. Yes, you are always welcome, my dear. Eleanor, when the day comes that you and yours sit with me at my own table, I shall rejoice with all my heart. (AUNT C. *and* NAN *exeunt.*)

POLLY (*arm about* MRS. G.). Don't feel badly, mother, dear. Every thing will come out right, I am sure of it. Come with me and we will watch the girls in the dairy. Some of them are trying to make butter.

MRS. G. Polly, be thoughtful of your sister Helen. She is so unhappy.

POLLY. Don't you think at she would let me join the club of King's Daughters now?

MRS. G. (*kisses her*). You have, at heart, always been one of them. (*Exeunt.*)

(*Enter* MISS REBECCA.)

REBECCA. The dear deacon has spoken at last, but I must hear from my unknown lover first. (*Sees hat and boots.*) Oh, what do I see? My Romeo hanging there? (*Crosses to tree.*) No, once more, I breathe. He was awakened from his refreshing slumber, and has doubtless wandered to the babbling brook, where, in its sylvan solitude, he may quench his thirst. A bit of paper peeping from his pocket. It may be a fond epistle for me. (*Takes paper from pocket;* GIRLS *heard laughing; thrusts paper back again.*) The girls are coming. They must not see me here. (*Hides behind tree.*)

(*Enter* GIRLS *laughing.*)

FLORENCE. It is the best joke. (*Points to hat and boots.*) Behold our Romeo. (GIRLS *laugh.*)

SALLIE. That is all that is left of him.

FLORENCE. I told you that his end would be spontaneous combustion.

SALLIE. Miss Rebecca is probably awaiting our coming with a trembling heart.

MABEL. My fond missives from Romeo to Deacon Starr and from Romeo to Miss Rebecca are accomplishing good work. The Deacon's curls rest becomingly every evening now upon the slumber pillow which makes Miss Rebecca's easy chair so comfortable.

KITTY. Miss Rebecca is a perfect symphony in pink. She has worn that color ever since we told her that Deacon Starr was fond of that color.

BETH. It is a pity to deceive her any longer. We ought to tell her that her Romeo is but the creation of Mab's intellect.

(MISS REBECCA *appears, very angry.*)

REBECCA. " Creation of Mab's intellect," indeed ! So you have been making fun of me, have you ?

GIRLS. Miss Rebecca !

REBECCA. Yes, I overheard your conversation. You have made me the laughing stock of the whole neighborhood.

KITTY. We didn't mean any harm, dear Miss Rebecca. (*Places hand soothingly upon* MISS R'S. *arm.*)

REBECCA (*throws off hand*). Don't " Dear Miss Rebecca " me. You are a set of mischief-making girls. You ought to be ashamed of yourselves. (*Shakes parasol at them.*)

FLORENCE. We thought only of your happiness.

REBECCA. My happiness indeed ! Only an excuse for that girl (*points parasol at* MABEL), who thinks herself a rising literary comet, to find something to write about. Your fathers shall respectively and collectively be informed of this outrage. (*Opens parasol with energy ; speaks dramatically.*) Beware of the ire of Rebecca Spencer. (*Exit.*)

BETH. Well, we've made a mess of it.

MABEL (*walks about with dignity*). Please treat me with proper respect, girls. It isn't every day that a comet comes down to earth dressed as a dairy maid. I always knew that some day I would make a sensation, and here I am. (GIRLS *laugh.*) A new discovery by Rebecca Spencer, spinster — a literary comet.

KITTY. She will never forgive us.

SALLIE. I think it just the best thing that could happen. The knowledge that another man loved his sweetheart has awakened the Deacon to a realizing sense of the true state of affairs, and I am willing to wager that Miss Rebecca will be engaged before the sun goes down, and the Club of King's Daughters can establish a new department in their work.

BETH. What will that be ?

SALLIE. A matrimonial agency. (GIRLS *laugh.*)

(*Enter* HELEN GRAHAM.)

KITTY. Well, Helen Graham, this is a nice time of day to present yourself at a hay-making party; never knew you to shirk work before.

FLORENCE. I am glad that you have on your costume, anyway. Why didn't you come before?

HELEN. Because I hadn't the heart to.

SALLIE (*arm about* HELEN). What is the matter with you? You ought to tell your friends and let them help you. That is what our club is for.

HELEN. Don't speak of the King's Daughters to me. I have no right to call myself one of them.

KITTY. Why, what do you mean? I am sure there is no one more ready to sew for the poor than you are.

HELEN. Ah, girls, I have learned another meaning of a King's Daughter. (*Does not see* NAN *and* POLLY, *who enter.*) You all know how unkind I was to my cousin Nan. I was selfish and hateful to her always. Jealous, fearful that she should have some of the pleasures that came to me. I will never again call myself a King's Daughter until she has forgiven me. (*Sinks upon mound at* L., *and buries face in hands.*)

NAN (*motions for* GIRLS *to leave the stage; all do so but* POLLY, *who remains at back;* NAN *comes down; soft music*). Helen.

HELEN (*raises head; rises*). Nan!

NAN. If you are so desirous of my forgiveness, Helen, why have you never sought me to ask for it. I have been away from your house a whole month, and this is the first time we have spoken.

HELEN (*holds head down*). I was ashamed to see you after my unkindness. ·

NAN. For ten years you treated me as one who had no right to receive a loving word. I was expected to run at your beck and call. (*Bitterly.*) When my usefulness was beyond your reach, you began to think of me a little.

HELEN. Spare me, Nan. I know that I deserve all this, but I am sorry for what I have done and humbly beg your pardon. (POLLY *shows signs of delight.*)

NAN. I can never forgive you. There is too much to forget.

HELEN. I have no right to expect it. (*Goes up stage.*)

POLLY (*comes down to* NAN). It is your birthday, Nannie, dear.

NAN. Yes, but the bitterness and humiliation of all those years cannot be wiped out in a moment.

POLLY. Cannot you forgive "*In His Name*"?

NAN (*hesitates; finally slowly turns and holds out hands to* HELEN). Helen!

HELEN (*runs down to her*). Nan, you will forgive me?

NAN. With my whole heart. (*They embrace.*)

HELEN. And my hatefulness about the letter?

NAN. What letter? (POLLY *tries to attract* HELEN'S *attention*.)

HELEN. The letter which you received from the school committee.

NAN. I don't understand. Polly found it in her pocket, where it had been all the time.

POLLY (*stands beside* HELEN). Yes, it had slipped down between my dress and the lining. (*Looks at* HELEN *with meaning*.)

HELEN. What do you mean, Polly Graham? (POLLY *motions her to be silent*.) No, I cannot be silent. I must speak. Polly dropped the letter, I found it and kept it.

NAN (*with amazement*). Cousin Helen!

HELEN. Do you wonder that I have not known a peaceful moment since you left us? Jealous that you should have a secret from me, I was determined to let you wait for the letter until too late for the appointment.

NAN. Oh, Helen! How could you do such a thing?

HELEN. I was selfish and hateful. (*Turns to* POLLY.) Why did you not tell Nan the truth?

POLLY. I knew the day would come when you would regret having done such a thing. I wanted to help you and be a King's Daughter.

HELEN. Oh, Polly! (*Bursts into tears*.)

POLLY (*arm about her*). Don't cry, Helen. Nan, won't you kiss and be friends?

NAN (*kisses* HELEN). Such friends, I hope, as we have never been before. (NAN *and* HELEN *walk to back of stage*.)

POLLY (*wipes eyes*). Guess there isn't any doubt about my being a King's Daughter *now*. (*Walks back and forth with dignity, singing "I'm so toppy*.")

(*Enter* KITTY *running*.)

KITTY. Oh, girls, do hurry. We are forming the march for the dance now.

HELEN (*holds out hands to* NAN *and* POLLY). We have two new members in our club, Kitty.

KITTY. Who are they?

HELEN. Nan and Polly.

KITTY. Three cheers for the new members. Come, the girls will be here in a few moments.

HELEN. Nan, this grand fête must be to celebrate your birthday. We will dance to many returns of it. (*Exeunt*.)

(*Enter* AUNT CLARISSA, R ; *looks off, watches* GIRLS.)

AUNT C. Nan and Helen together. A good omen. No better birthday gift for my dear girl than such a reconciliation. My little method of deception has proved a success. Nan loves me for myself, Polly was always pure gold, and Helen will be a better and nobler woman for these days of repentance.

(*Enter* MISS REBECCA; *walks quickly across stage.*)

AUNT C. Where are you going in such a hurry? You seem to be in great excitement. Can I do any thing for you?

REBECCA. I have been shamefully abused. My affairs have been made common talk by those heedless, fun-loving girls. Being a creature of impulse, I am seeking revenge.

AUNT C. I don't understand.

REBECCA (*with sarcasm*). Ask any of the King's Daughters, whose mission it is to perform noble deeds. They will tell you. (*Exit.*)

AUNT C. Something serious must have happened to make the usually placid Miss Rebecca so excited. I wonder what it can be?

(*Enter* NAN *and* POLLY.)

POLLY. The girls are coming. It is a lovely sight.

AUNT C. Why are not you and Nan in the dance?

NAN. We didn't have time to put on the costumes. We will sit beside you and watch it. (GIRLS *seated by* AUNT C. *on mound* L.)

(*Music;* GIRLS *march on and give the "Dairy Maid March and Dance." It will be necessary to introduce others for this.* GIRLS *march off after dance.*)

POLLY. I mean to try my hand at churning butter. I have been dying to, all day. (*Exit.*)

NAN. Don't you think that the girls are a success as dairy maids?

AUNT C. It was a perfect picture. How much pleasure this unknown hostess is giving you all.

NAN. And to think that this should happen on my birthday. Best of all, Helen and I are friends. My cup of joy would be overflowing, if I could go to the ball to-night.

AUNT C. Why not?

NAN. My best gown is not suitable for such an affair.

AUNT C. I have made you no gift upon your birthday. Did you think that I had forgotten you?

NAN. You and I do not need gifts to remind us of one another. How happy we have been in our little cottage!

AUNT C. Yes, but you work so hard.

NAN. What of that? I know a rich reward is awaiting me at home. (*Kisses her.*) My Aunt Clarissa.

AUNT C. And do you never long for riches?

NAN. We all love beautiful things; but if riches had been my portion, you and I would never have found how dearly we loved one another.

AUNT C. (*both rise;* GIRLS *come on, during this conversation, and remain at back of stage*). I have a birthday gift for you, my dear. Let me be the fairy godmother and send you to the ball to-night. You will find a Cinderella gown at home ; put it on and dance to your heart's content. (GIRLS *come down.*) I shall be proud to have our hostess meet the King's Daughters. They are such well bred girls.

(*Enter* POLLY ; *wears large apron, which is covered with cream.*)

POLLY. I'm well bred and buttered now. (*Makes wry face ;* GIRLS *laugh.*) Just look at me. Did you ever see such a sight. The cream went all over me. Some one lend me a handkerchief.

KITTY. Dairy maids never carry one.

AUNT C. And mine has been left at home.

NAN (*who through the first part of this act carries old fashioned bonnet on arm*). We can take the lining of this old bonnet. (*Tears out lining ; paper falls out.*)

KITTY (*picks up paper*). Nan, we have caught you this time. A novel way of hiding your love letters.

NAN (*takes letter*). What can it be ? Uncle John's will. (*Crosses to* AUNT C.) What does this all mean, Aunt Clarissa ?

AUNT C. (*after reading paper*). It means, my dear, that when your Uncle John gave you the bonnet, and said it might prove a shelter for your head, his meaning was a double one. He has left you the bulk of his property.

NAN. This wealth will be mine ?

AUNT C. Yes, you are an heiress.

KITTY. Three cheers for Nan, the heiress. (GIRLS *cheer.*)

HELEN (*crosses to* NAN). I am so glad for you. (*To* AUNT C.) Aunt Clarissa, Nan has forgiven me. Will you ?

AUNT C. (*gives her hand*). Yes, my dear. Only too glad that you have proved better at heart than you seemed.

(*Enter* MRS. GRAHAM.)

FLORENCE. Oh, Mrs. Graham ! Have you heard the good news ?

MRS. G. What is it ?

HELEN. Nan found Uncle John's will beneath the lining of her bonnet. He has left a fortune to her.

MRS. G. (*gives hand to* NAN). I am indeed glad for your good fortune.

NAN. Thank you, Aunt Graham. Girls, come with me and see my birthday present from Aunt Clarissa.

GIRLS. Indeed we will. (*Exeunt.*)

MRS. G. Helen and Nan together ! Then this means —

AUNT C. Forgiveness and, I trust, future happiness.

MRS. G. My prayers have been answered. Will you make my home yours ?

AUNT C. Nan and I will always have our own fireside, but shall be glad of a welcome at yours.

MRS. G. Will you come now ?

AUNT C. Not yet, I have something to attend to first.

MRS. G. Let your coming be soon that I may not awaken and find this all a dream. (*Exit.*)

AUNT C. My little comedy is almost at an end. Only a few preparations for the final tableau. I will send a note to Nan. (*Takes paper and pencil from pocket; writes, encloses it in envelope, addresses it; leaves note upon mound.*) And now, poor Aunt Clarissa vanishes from the scene. (*Exit.*)

(*Enter* SALLIE *and* FLORENCE; SALLIE *has Kodak pictures.*)

FLORENCE. Isn't that gown of Nan's too lovely for anything. I thought that Aunt Clarissa was poor.

SALLIE. She seems to be, but that gown is a dream. Some of these pictures are rather good. (GIRLS *look at pictures together.*)

FLORENCE. Here is Polly eating cake. (*Laughs.*) Better of the cake than of Polly.

SALLIE. This is Polly posing as an artist. The picture seems to be in mourning.

FLORENCE. I don't wonder, so much black paint. Who is this?

SALLIE. That is a bird's eye view of Aunt Clarissa.

FLORENCE. She is at Helen's tea table; she has an envelope in her hand.

SALLIE. Didn't we find an envelope with some money in it on that very day and at that very table?

FLORENCE. We did. Put that and Nan's lovely gown together and I tell you there is some mystery here.

SALLIE. Nonsense; it couldn't be possible. We should have found it out in some way.

FLORENCE. You wait and see.

(*Enter* KITTY *and* BETH *with table; place it in* C. *of stage.*)

KITTY. It is decreed that we are to have our supper here.

(*Enter* RUTH *with table cover; spreads it over table.*)

RUTH. If we only had some young men here now, it would be perfect.

KITTY. Perfect what! *Bliss?*

(MABEL *enters with plates : others exeunt and bring in the rest of the dishes.*)

MABEL (*arranging table; sings*) :

" And we'll drink to the health of our favorite lass."

KITTY. That is a good idea. We will drink Nan's health on her birthday in lemonade.

RUTH. Who will make it?

MABEL. I will. (*Some of the* GIRLS *cut lemons ;* MABEL *prepares lemonade.*) Where is the sugar?

KITTY. Let your comet eyes look into it. That will be enough.

MABEL. "Comet eyes" is good. So long as you did not call them comic eyes, I will forgive you. (*Tastes it.*) There is a " more-ish " taste about that which would please Polly. Now, let's remove the *débris* and everything will soon be ready. (GIRLS *remove lemon peel, etc.*)

(*Enter* POLLY, *back to audience, bowing profoundly.*)

KITTY. Hail to our queen.

(*Enter* NAN, *wears white gown, simple but elegant ; wears* POLLY'S *roses.*)

RUTH. You look too sweet to live.

NAN. Don't say that, just when the fun is commencing. I must pinch myself to see if it isn't all a dream.

KITTY. It wouldn't be bad, even for a dream.

FLORENCE. You must have a fairy godmother somewhere, Nan. They say that everything goes by threes. You will have another surprise before the day is over, (*Takes letter from mound.*) What is this? More money for our poor. No, it is addressed to Nan.

KITTY. The surprise. Do open it, Nan.

NAN. It may not be pleasant news. I dread to open it. (*Opens it.*) From Aunt Clarissa.

HELEN (*looks at envelope*). The same handwriting.

NAN (*reads*). Dear Nan : Now that riches have come into your life, you will not need your poor Aunt Clarissa any longer. Let the coming hostess of Grafton Manse find the King's Daughters as worthy of her esteem as I have. Good-by. Your poor, but loving, Aunt Clarissa. (*Speaks.*) Oh, this is cruel. What would all the wealth of the world be to me without Aunt Clarissa ? She cannot have gone very far. I must find her.

(*Enter* MISS REBECCA.)

NAN. Have you seen Aunt Clarissa?

REBECCA. Yes, she was climbing the hill to yonder Manse.

NAN. Then I shall be in time. (*Runs to entrance,* R.)

REBECCA (*stops her*). You were not to follow. She has gone to pay her respects to our new hostess. She told me to tell you that she would see you again.

NAN. Then I will wait. Once within these loving arms, she will not leave me. But you seem troubled.

REBECCA. My very hair has turned white with chagrin and mortification with this day's work.

NAN. What do you mean?

REBECCA. Ask the King's Daughters. They will tell you.

FLORENCE. Only an attempt to make Miss Rebecca and the Deacon happy.

REBECCA. " Only an attempt." The day will come when every one of you will be sorry that you made such an attempt. I thirst for revenge.

FLORENCE. Still thirsty, and we have no soda to offer you. Girls, a glass of lemonade. (KITTY *brings lemonade;* MISS R. *refuses it.*)

MABEL. Let me read to you my latest production. That may be soothing.

REBECCA (*snatches paper from* MABEL; *tears it and throws it upon floor*). Spend your time in the study of the rules of common politeness. It will be more to your advantage.

MABEL. Miss Rebecca!

NAN. Enough of this. Girls, leave us for a few moments. Perhaps we can straighten this out. It seems to be a tangled web of misunderstanding.

POLLY. You always come to the rescue, Nan. I hope I shall have a love affair before you die.

NAN. Why, what could I do?

POLLY. We could have all the lovers' quarrels we pleased and you could make everything look like sunshine after it.

NAN. You flatterer. (GIRLS *exeunt.*)

REBECCA. Don't think that I shall ever forgive them. The wound is too deep.

NAN (*leads her to mound* R. ; *both sit*). Let me talk to you, Miss Rebecca. The mission of the King's Daughters is to do good.

REBECCA. I don't call it doing good to torment a poor, lone female like myself — to deceive me.

NAN. Deacon Starr has loved you all these years, and has never told you of it.

REBECCA. Not until to-day.

NAN. He has spoken, then. It is all the result of the girls' interest in you. It is because they have thought of you, felt sorry for you in your loneliness, that they have done this.

REBECCA. I thought that they were making sport of me.

NAN. Never! They respect you too highly for that. It was only for your happiness. (*Both rise.*) And if they gave themselves a little fun with it, remember that they are only girls and that to see the bright and jolly side of life is one of the prerogatives of youth. (*Gives hand to* MISS R.) I shall never forget how kind you have been to me, Miss Rebecca, and hope that on this my birthday you will celebrate it by giving an answer to Deacon Starr which will make it for him, as it has been for me, a red letter day.

REBECCA. He shall have it. Thank you for your kind words, and may this be but the beginning of a bright and happy future for you. (*Exit.*)

NAN. She will be happy now. What can Aunt Clarissa mean

by writing me such a note? This gown is too beautiful for her scanty purse. Everything seems surrounded in mystery.

(*Enter* GIRLS.)

KITTY. It is time for our hostess.

HELEN. I don't understand about that handwriting. Nan, could it have been Aunt Clarissa who has been giving us money?

KITTY. It is her handwriting.

NAN. But she had no money to give.

FLORENCE (*takes hold of* NAN'S *dress*). I am not so sure of that.

(POLLY *enters running.*)

POLLY. Oh, girls! A servant told us that our hostess was coming here to meet us.

KITTY. Here is the table spread for our tea. What shall we do with it?

FLORENCE. Let's place it at one side, and when she comes we will drink her health as well. (GIRLS *move table to side of stage.*)

POLLY (*looks off* L.). I do believe that she is coming now. (GIRLS *rush to* POLLY; *all crowd and try to see.*) Don't push me into her very arms.

KITTY. The servants are standing in a line on either side; see them bow.

RUTH. Can you see her?

POLLY. Yes, there she comes; but I can't see her face.

FLORENCE. We do not need to see her face to be assured of its loveliness.

NAN. I wish Aunt Clarissa were here.

(*Enter* MRS. GRAHAM.)

POLLY. Oh, mamma! The mistress of Grafton Manse is coming.

MRS. G. She will receive a royal welcome.

HELEN. How could it be otherwise from the King's Daughters?

POLLY. I can hear the rustle of her silk gown.

KITTY. Here she is Stand in a row and receive her with due respect. (GIRLS *form on either side of stage.*)

(*Enter* AUNT CLARISSA, *richly dressed.*)

GIRLS. Aunt Clarissa!

AUNT C. The new mistress of Grafton Manse, if you please.

NAN (*goes to her*). You, mistress of Grafton Manse?

AUNT C. Yes.

KITTY. The fairy godmother.

AUNT C. Eleanor, you will forgive me for this masquerading, but I wished to know who would love me for myself. My property was not lost through speculations; and as I wished to make some one my heir, I took this means.

NAN. And you deceived me, too. Well, this is a day of surprises.

KITTY. Then Nan will be a double heiress.

AUNT C. I thought to find one by my deception, but my discovery proved richer than I dared hope. Nan, who because she knew what loneliness was, gave me all that she possessed. (*Holds out hand to* POLLY.) Polly, who proved herself Nan's champion and was always loyal. (*Holds out hand to* HELEN.) And Helen, who stumbled and walked blindly, until her eyes were opened to the true sense of giving. Am I not rich in finding all these treasures? All shall share alike.

MRS. G. You are too kind to us.

HELEN. I do not deserve all this, Aunt Clarissa.

AUNT C. Let your future life prove that you do.

HELEN. The money given to us.

AUNT C. (*laughing*). I was the guilty party.

NAN. And I would not let you give when you wished to.

AUNT C. It went with the masquerading, my dear.

(*Enter* MISS REBECCA.)

KITTY. Miss Rebecca!

REBECCA. The affianced bride of Deacon Starr, if you please.

MABEL. Our congratulations. (GIRLS *gather about her and offer congratulations.*)

NAN. Your note, Aunt Clarissa. I read between the lines now. I was only bidding good-by to the one who helped me to share poverty and hard work.

AUNT C. The life was a hard one, but the coming one of plenty will be all the sweeter to you.

KITTY. We must drink the health of our new hostess.

GIRLS. Oh, yes! (*Fill glasses; all stand with them in hand.*)

MABEL. The health of our hostess, who comes amongst us as an old and tried friend. Peace and happiness to Aunt Clarissa. (*All raise glasses to lips.*)

MABEL (*To* NAN). Many happy returns of this her birthday. (*Same business.*)

AUNT C. Let me offer a toast to the King's Daughters. May their noble work continue: helping the needy "In His name"; giving because it is good to give; and may every young woman who seeks to live an honest, upright life find the "Open Sesamè" to peace and happiness in becoming truly, a King's Daughter.

(*Tableau;* All *stand with glasses raised;* AUNT CLARISSA, NAN, POLLY, *and* MRS. G., *in* C.; GIRLS *and* MISS REBECCA *grouped on either side.*

SLOW CURTAIN.

NOTE. — "Dairy Maid's March and Dance" can be found at publishers, price, 25 cents; also the song, "The King's Daughters," price, 30 cents.

www.ingramcontent.com/pod-product-compliance
Lightning Source LLC
Chambersburg PA
CBHW031749090426
42739CB00008B/942